SWINGERS

SWINGERS
Jon Favreau
also
THE SWINGERS RULES
Vince Vaughn and Jon Favreau

With a Preface by
JON FAVREAU

faber and faber

First published in the United States in 1997
by Miramax Books/Hyperion

First published in the United Kingdom in 2000
by Faber and Faber Limited,
3 Queen Square London WC1N 3AU
Published by arrangement with Hyperion, 114 Fifth Avenue,
New York, New York 10011, U.S.A.

Printed in England by
Mackays of Chatham plc, Chatham, Kent

Jon Favreau is hereby identified as author of this work in accordance
with Section 77 of the Copyright, Designs and Patents Act 1988

A CIP record for this book is available from the British Library

ISBN 0 571-20310-8

2 4 6 8 10 9 7 5 3 1

CONTENTS

preface

When I wrote *Swingers,* I never thought anyone would read it but my friends. It was my first screenplay, and I banged it out in less than two weeks. My friends read it. They got a big kick out of it. I had purposely based the characters on them, and exaggerated their most ridiculous characteristics to the point of absurdity. To be fair, I did the same to myself.

I showed it to my agent. She sent it out. Someone wanted to buy it. I hadn't had a real acting gig in a long time and was excited about the prospect of having a produced screenplay under my belt. I was promised a lead role and a producing credit to boot. I went to my first story meeting with bells on.

They wanted to change everything. I mean, everything. They wanted to set it in Vegas. They wanted a female in one of the main roles. They wanted less Trent. They wanted more violence. They wanted to cut out all the "money's" and "baby's." They wanted a movie that wasn't *Swingers.*

I set up a staged reading (with the actors I based it on) in order to show them the dialogue *could* work, and to present my friends in the best possible light as casting possibilities.

The reading killed. I have to honestly say it was as funny, if not more, than the film. This was the dream cast. All we needed was a camera to shoot it. My agent said we're pulling the deal. It was that day we set out to make it ourselves.

Nicole LaLoggia did budgets, her producing partner Victor Simpkins did proposals, and the actors did readings. For two years we heard how great it was. For two years we heard that we needed a name to sell video boxes in order to justify the budget. It had gotten to the point where I could've directed it and starred in it if we recast the supporting roles. Something about it didn't seem right. Then Doug came along.

Doug Liman was Nicole's friend and roommate. I knew him from around the way. He presented me with an interesting proposition. He had access to a quarter of a million through a private investor and felt it was enough to shoot the script as written. This was about a fifth of our original budget, so I took pause. He assured me that it was possible with a little ingenuity. Victor and Nicole had worked with him before and stood by his opinion. I took the dive. The next day we were in preproduction.

Shooting was hell, but I had my cast. They knew their roles inside and out from the staged readings.

Editing was also hell. It was a mad rush for the Sundance deadline. We had no money or time for "post," but the fact that we all collaborated from day one made the most of our limited resources. We looked at Steve Mirrione's first assembly, and dove right into it. A week later, Victor and Nicole planted themselves on the couch of the editing room, and we didn't stop until we got it right. Together we picked the music that worked and, thanks to music supervisor Julianne Kelly, could afford. Next thing I knew, we had a movie, but Sundance passed. The tape and sound were too rough to be appreciated, and entire sequences were not yet finished.

Miramax bought it anyway. We took the money and threw a party where we paid our crew their deferred salaries. We also bought the music rights and gave the film a postproduction polish. We were ready for the festivals.

First was Venice, then Telluride, then Toronto, then Boston and Chicago. It was a whirlwind tour. We showed *Swingers* all over the world and the people laughed.

Press became a full-time job. Everyone wanted to know everything. There wasn't much to tell. We weren't trying to make *Gone With the Wind*. We just wanted to make a movie as best we could with what we had. We got real lucky it turned out well, and even luckier that it was so well received. The most important thing to us was that we were proud of it.

The question the press asked most was about the "rules" of dating that the film presents. For some reason, everyone is obsessed with "rules" these days. The character of Mike is also obsessed with "rules" in *Swingers,* because he feels so powerless in the new and vulnerable world of dating. The film demonstrates several "rules," and I'm always asked to elaborate on them. We thought it might be fun to include a companion guide to break it down for those of you who want the real, so Vince and I put together a chapter on the rules of dating.

The screenplay has for the most part been presented as it was originally written. Although I incorporated some last minute production rewrites, I resisted the temptation of amending the script to reflect the way the film was cut. As a result, there are some lines that never made it to the big screen and improvised dialogue was intentionally omitted. This is most clear in some of Trent's monologues and the presence of the answering machine as a recurring character. Many of the music cues have also changed. Keep your eye out for gags and shots that we didn't have the time or money to film.

INT. HOLLYWOOD HILLS DINER—BOOTH IN FRONT WINDOW—NIGHT

Rob sits across from Mike.

> **MIKE**
> And what if I don't want to give up on her?

> **ROB**
> You don't call.

> **MIKE**
> But you said I shouldn't call if I *wanted* to give up on her.

> **ROB**
> Right.

> **MIKE**
> So I don't call either way.

> **ROB**
> Right.

> **MIKE**
> So what's the difference?

> **ROB**
> The only difference between giving up and not giving up is if you take her back when she wants to come back. See, you can't do anything to make her want to come back. You can only do things to make her not want to come back.

> **MIKE**
> So the only difference is if I forget about her or pretend to forget about her.

ROB

Right.

MIKE

Well *that* sucks.

ROB

It sucks.

MIKE

So it's almost a retroactive decision. So I could, like, let's say, forget about her and when she comes back make like I just pretended to forget about her.

ROB

Right . . . or more likely the opposite.

MIKE

Right . . . Wait, what do you mean?

ROB

I mean at first you'll pretend not to care, not call—whatever, and then, eventually, you really won't care.

MIKE

Unless she comes back first.

ROB

Ah, see, that's the thing. Somehow they don't come back until you really don't care anymore.

MIKE

There's the rub.

ROB

There's the rub.

MIKE

Thanks, man. Sorry we always talk about the same thing all the time . . .

ROB
Hey man, don't sweat it.

MIKE
It's just that you've been there. Your advice really helps.

ROB
No problem.

MIKE
Rob, I just want you to know, you're the only one I can talk to about her.

ROB
Thanks. Thanks, man.

CUT TO:
INT. MIKE'S APARTMENT—NIGHT

CLOSE-UP on answering machine. Mike pushes the button.

ANSWERING MACHINE
(synthesized voice)
Hello, you have *five* messages.

Mike's eyes light up. He paces in anticipation as the tape rewinds.

ANSWERING MACHINE
(male voice)
Hey, baby. It's Trent. You gotta get that girl out of your head. I hope my advice helped . . .

Mike fastforwards to next message.

ANSWERING MACHINE
(synthesized voice)
Skipping message.
(male voice)

What's up, Mike. If you want to talk some more about Michelle . . .
> *(synthesized voice)*

Skipping message.
> *(female voice)*
> Mike, it's Chris. Feeling better yet about. . . ?
> *(synthesized voice)*
> Skipping message.

Tension grows with every inch of spooling tape. Did she leave a message?

ANSWERING MACHINE
> *(female voice)*
> Hi, Mike. Did she call yet? I'm sure she . . .
> *(synthesized voice)*
> Skipping message.

The last one. It's a long shot, but he's got the faith.

ANSWERING MACHINE
> *(elderly female voice)*
> Michael, this is Grandma. We all miss you back here in New York. Please call. You still haven't told me if you got the part on that television program. I told the whole family and they're very excited to know if . . .
> *(synthesized voice)*
> Skipping message. End of final message.

MIKE
> *(lighting a cigarette, defeated)*
> Shit.

ANSWERING MACHINE
> *(synthesized voice)*
> You have to put things in perspective.

MIKE
> *(unfazed by the sentient appliance)*
> I know, I know.

ANSWERING MACHINE
(synthesized voice)

She doesn't deserve you.

MIKE

Thanks. I appreciate that.

ANSWERING MACHINE
(synthesized voice)

There's plenty of fish in the sea.

MIKE

Okay. I'll think about that. Bye.

ANSWERING MACHINE
(synthesized voice)

Life, after all . . .

MIKE
(growing irate)

Enough. I've got to use the phone.

ANSWERING MACHINE
(synthesized voice)

Are you calling *her*?

MIKE

No. Stop, come on.

The LED goes black as the machine beeps off. Mike picks up the phone and hits autodial.

Phone rings again, then is answered.

TRENT
(over phone)

Hello?

MIKE

S'up Trent?

TRENT

Lemme get off the other line, baby.

We hear the clicks of call-waiting-hold limbo.

TRENT
(returning to line)

That was Sue. We got two parties tonight. One's for a modeling agency.

MIKE

I don't know . . .

TRENT

Listen to me, baby, there are going to be beautiful babies there.

MIKE

Trent, I don't feel like going out tonight. I got shit to do tomorrow . . .

TRENT

Listen to you. I got a final callback for a pilot at nine and I'm going. You gotta get out with some beautiful babies. You can't sit home thinking about her.

MIKE

I don't know . . .

TRENT

I don't know, I don't know—listen to you. We're gonna have fun tonight. We gotta get you out of that stuffy apartment.

MIKE

We're gonna spend half the night driving around the Hills looking for one party and then leaving 'cause it sucks, then we're gonna look for this other party you heard about. But, Trent, all the parties and bars, they all suck. I spend half the night trying to talk to some girl who's eyes are darting around to see if there's someone else she should be talking to. And it's like I'm supposed to be all happy cause she's wearing a backpack. Half of them are nasty skanks who wouldn't be shit if they weren't surrounded by a bunch of drunken horny assholes. I'm not gonna be one of those assholes. I want to throw up. Some fuckin' *skank* who isn't half the woman my girlfriend is is gonna front *me*? It makes me want to fuckin' puke.

TRENT
(beat)
Shut up. Jesus Christ. We gotta get you the fuck outta Dodge. We're going to Vegas.

MIKE
What are you talking about? Vegas?

TRENT
Vegas.

MIKE
What Vegas?

TRENT
We're going to Vegas.

MIKE
When?

TRENT
Tonight, baby.

MIKE
Are you *listening* to me?

TRENT
I'll pick you up in a half hour.

MIKE
I'm not going to Vegas.

TRENT

Shut up—yes you are. Now listen to Tee. We'll stop at a cash machine on the way.

MIKE

I'm not going to Vegas.

SMASH CUT TO:
INT. TRENT'S CAR—NIGHT

MIKE
(counting bills)
I can't lose more than a hundred.

INT. TRENT'S CAR—DETAIL
SHOT—SPEEDOMETER—NIGHT

The NEEDLE IS PINNED. The gauges are blurred by the vibration of the poorly tuned engine. The SHOT WIDENS to reveal that the "Oil" and "Service" dummy lights are both illuminated, casting an eerie red glow onto TRENT's white knuckles. A parking ticket is under the wiper of the '64 Comet convertible.

EXT. DESERT ROAD—NIGHT

Trent's car is red-lined. They blow past cars like they were standing still. The SWINGERS are Vegas bound. Do not pass go.

INT. TRENT'S CAR—NIGHT

MIKE

Now listen, I took out three hundred, but I'm only
gonna bet with one. I figure if we buy a lot of chips,
the pit boss will see and they'll comp us all sorts of shit,
then we trade back the chips at the end of the night.
You gotta be cool though.

TRENT

I'm cool, baby. They're gonna give Daddy a room,
some breakfast, maybe Bennett's singing.

MIKE

What are you wearing? I thought we said we were
gonna wear suits.

TRENT

Will you stop worrying about everything?

MIKE

No, seriously, if you're dressed nice and you act like
you gamble a lot, they give you free shit.

TRENT

Don't worry, it's in the back. I'll change when we get
there.

MIKE

Uh-uh. No way. We gotta show up wearing them if
this is gonna work. I'm telling you, they're watching
you from the minute you drive up.

TRENT

All right already. I'll put it on.

*Mike grabs the wheel with his left hand and replaces Trent's foot on the
accelerator without missing a beat. Trent twists around and pulls his dry-
cleaned suit out of the backseat and tears away the plastic. He begins to dress
awkwardly in the driver's seat. The car continues to barrel past all traffic on
the freeway, swerving violently.*

MIKE

I'm serious. This is how you do it. I'm telling you.

TRENT

I know. Daddy's gonna get the *Rainman* suite. Vegas,
baby. We're going to Vegas!

MIKE

Vegas! You think we'll get there by midnight?

TRENT

Baby, we're gonna be up five hundy by midnight.
Vegas, baby!

MIKE

Vegas!

Mike twists up the Chairman of the Board as we . . .

DISSOLVE TO:
INT. TRENT'S CAR—HOURS LATER

*The two swingers are starting to fray around the edges but are unwilling to
admit it to each other or themselves. Trent is fully dressed. Frank has been
replaced by talk radio.*

TRENT

Vegas, baby!

MIKE

Vegas!

The needle is still buried.

DISSOLVE TO:
**INT. TRENT'S CAR—MANY HOURS
LATER**

*Sleep deprivation and desert static radio. Loosened collars. Fast-food wrappers
on the dash.*

TRENT

Vegas.

MIKE

Vegas.

DISSOLVE TO:
INT. TRENT'S CAR—LATER THAT NIGHT

Mike is sleeping in the passenger seat.

TRENT

Wake up, baby.

MIKE
(stirring)

Whu?

TRENT

Look at it, baby. Vegas, baby!

Trent points out a mountain range. It is now the only thing separating them from their destination. The surreal glow of the desert sky is accentuated by the unnatural slashing of the cobalt and ruby lasers emanating from a source masked by the craggy peaks. Mike slowly stirs from his slumber. He is transfixed by this affrontation of nature. It is his first glimpse of the city without God.

MIKE
(in reverie)

Vegas.

CUT TO:
EXT. VEGAS STRIP—NIGHT

The shrill cry of Basie's fat brass section heralds the arrival of the young swingers. Their eyes drink every watt of golden light as Sinatra's crooning urges them on.

The convertible top motors down as the Comet makes a leisurely left turn onto the main drag. The swingers bask in the man-made daylight.

Mike has either had enough sleep or so little that it no longer matters. Either way, there's no turning back.

They roll up to a casino valet.

CUT TO:
EXT. VEGAS STRIP—NIGHT

DETAIL INSERT of "dice" valve cap on Trent's tire as it settles to a stop in the casino's driveway.

EXT. STARDUST VALET—VEGAS STRIP—NIGHT

TILT UP from buffed shoes to reveal Mike dressed to the nines in classic vintage threads. He's trying to look at ease as he straightens his cuff links. He approaches Trent, who suavely leans against his worn-down ride. He's a tall, slim, good-looking cat. His sharkskin suit hangs well on his lanky frame as it tapers to his ankles. He tosses keys to the VALET. All fourteen of Basie's horns scream. The swingers exchange a suave nod and enter the casino without saying a word. Maybe this isn't such a bad idea.

INT. CASINO—NIGHT

> **MIKE**
> I thought Caesar's was the dope spot.

> **TRENT**
> Back in the day this place was a contender. Now they

appreciate the business. They'll fall all over themselves
for class clientele like us. You want to be fresh on the
scene, right, baby?

MIKE

What about the new places down the strip?

TRENT

Trust me, Mikey, you don't want that Pirates of the
Caribbean shit. Or fuckin' rock-and-roll grunge vibe.
Cats like us gotta kick it old school.

MIKE

This place is dead. I thought this was the city that never
sleeps.

TRENT

That's New York, baby. You should know that. Where
are the waitresses? I'm gonna find me two and pull a
"Fredo."

MIKE

They're all skanks.

TRENT

Baby, there are beautiful babies here.

MIKE

Tee, the beautiful babies don't work Wednesdays
midnight to six. This is the skank shift.

TRENT

What are you talking about? Look at all the honeys.

*Trent accosts a cute WAITRESS (CHRISTY) who passes with a tray of
drinks.*

TRENT
(pointing to Mike)
Remember this face, darling. He's the man behind the
man *behind* the man.

The waitress cracks a smile as she crosses away. Mike is visibly embarrassed.

MIKE

Cut that shit out.

TRENT

She smiled, baby.

MIKE

That's not cool.

TRENT

Did she, or did she not smile?

MIKE

It doesn't matter . . .

TRENT

I'm telling you, they love that shit.

MIKE

You're gonna screw up our plan.

TRENT

We're gonna get laid, baby.

MIKE

First let's see what happens if we play it cool.

TRENT

What? You think she's gonna tell her pit boss on us?

MIKE

Don't make fun, I think we can get some free shit if we don't fuck around.

TRENT

Who's fucking around? I'm not making fun. Let's do it, baby.

MIKE

The trick is to look like you don't need it, then they give you shit for free.

TRENT

Well, you look *money*, baby. We both look *money*.

Mike points to a semicurtained, semi-roped-off area near the baccarat tables. The clientele is classier, but they're still obviously overdressed.

MIKE
(pointing)
That's where we make our scene.

TRENT

You think they're watching?

MIKE

Oh, they're watching all right. They're watching.

CUT TO:
INT. CASINO—THE CLASSY
SECTION—NIGHT

Mike is at a blackjack table with Trent at his side. The game has paused to observe the newcomers as Mike draws a billfold out of his breast pocket. They're pulling it off with only slightly noticeable effort.

MIKE

I don't know, I guess I'll *start* with three hundred in, uh, blacks.

Mike tries to hand the DEALER a handful of twenties after counting them twice.

DEALER

On the table.

MIKE

Sorry?

DEALER

You have to lay it on the table.

MIKE

Uh, I don't want to bet it all.

The other players grow impatient.

DEALER

You're not allowed to hand me money, sir. You'll have
to lay it on the table if you want me to change it.

MIKE
(hastily laying down the bills)
Oh . . . right.

*The dealer lays out the bills such that the amount is visible to the camera
encased in the black glass globe overhead.*

*The dealer chirps out an unintelligible formality and the PIT BOSS chirps
the response. Trent and Mike stare at the pit boss ten feet away.*

*The dealer plunks down the measly THREE CHIPS, which represent
Mike's entire cash reserve. Not quite the effect he had hoped for.*

*The swingers stare at the chips. The players stare at the swingers. The dealer
stares at the pit boss.*

MIKE

Do you have anything smaller?

DEALER

Yes, but I'm afraid this table has a hundred-dollar-
minimum bet. Perhaps you'd be more comfortable at
one of our lower-stakes-tables.

*The dealer indicates a FIVE-DOLLAR TABLE across the room where a
disheveled DEALER deals to a BLUEHAIR, a BIKER, and a COUPLE
in matching Siegfried and Roy T-shirts.*

The swingers look back to the dealer, who is now flanked by the pit boss.

The tense silence is broken by . . .

CHRISTY

Drinks?

(then to Mike)

"Man behind the man?"

Trent looks over to see that it's the same WAITRESS who flashed him a smile earlier.

MIKE

Yes, I'll have a scotch on the rocks, please. Anything will do. As long as it's not a blend, of course. Any single malt. A Glenlivet or Glenfiddich, perhaps. Maybe a Glengowen. Any "Glen."

CHRISTY

(under her breath)

One scotch on the rocks.

She leaves. Mike regains his composure.

Mike throws a chip in the circle. Trent is shocked. That's a hundred bucks. Mike and Trent share a look. The dealer and the pit boss exchange glances. Bets are all down and the cards are meticulously dealt.

The dealer has a two showing. Mike has been dealt a six and a five—eleven.

TRENT

(hushed tones)

Double down.

MIKE

(even husheder)

What?!?

TRENT

Double down, baby. You gotta double down on an eleven.

MIKE

I know, but—

TRENT

You gotta do it.

MIKE

. . . but that's *two hundred dollars.* This is *blood money* . . .

TRENT

If we don't look like we know what we're doing, then we may as well . . .

Everyone's waiting for them.

MIKE

I know.

The dealer, the pit boss, and all the players look on as Mike drops ANOTHER BLACK CHIP in the circle with a barely audible, yet deafening, thud.

MIKE
(*with all the nonchalance he can muster*)
Double down.

A bead of sweat.

The sharp snap of a dealt card.

It's a seven. Eighteen.

Disappointment twists their faces.

Finally the dealer flips over his card.

It's a king! Twelve. *Here comes the bust* . . .

Flick- four. Sixteen! *Here comes the bust* . . .

Flick- five. Twenty one. *Groans all around, except for the swingers who watch their chips slide away in silence.*

Mike breaks the spell with a plucky smile from the pit of his stomach.

MIKE
(to the pit boss)
Sure can use some dinner about now.

SMASH CUT TO:

Trent and Mike are wedged between the BLUEHAIR and the BIKER at the FIVE-DOLLAR TABLE. They share a pile of red chips.

TRENT
I'm telling you, baby, you *always* double down on an eleven.

MIKE
Yeah? Well obviously not *always*!

TRENT
Always, baby.

MIKE
I'm just saying, not in this particular case.

TRENT
Always.

MIKE
But I *lost*! How can you say *always*?!?

In the meantime, the bluehair has been dealt an eleven. *This captures the swingers' attention.*

BLUEHAIR
Hit.

Four. Fifteen all together.

BLUEHAIR
Oh . . . I don't know . . . Hit.

Two. Seventeen. Dealer has a seven showing.

BLUEHAIR

What the hell—hit.

Four! Twenty-one.

DEALER 2
(with a warm smile)
Twenty-one. Congratulations.

Polite applause from around the table, which the Bluehair humbly waves off. Mike looks at Trent. Daggers. Trent shrugs.

The PIT BOSS approaches.

PIT BOSS
Would you care for some breakfast, ma'am?

BLUEHAIR
Well . . . ? No, I shouldn't. Maybe later. Thank you, though.

MIKE
(to Trent, under his breath)
I'm gonna *kill* you.

CUT TO:
**INT. CASINO—CASHIER'S
WINDOW—NIGHT**

Mike is presented a stack of twenties by the CASHIER, who counts them out. Trent looks on. Mike turns to go. Trent struggles to cheer him up.

TRENT
What's that? One-twenty? You're up twenty bucks, baby.

Mike throws him a disgusted glare.

TRENT

. . . Well, you know, not counting the first table.

MIKE

Thanks for clarifying that.

TRENT

Hey, man, I'm down too, you know.

MIKE

Yeah, how much?

TRENT

I don't know, what? Thirty, forty maybe.

MIKE

Don't give me that shit. You know exactly how much
you lost. What'd you drop?

TRENT

Twenty . . . but I was down at least fifty. I'm sorry, I
got hot at the crap table.

MIKE

You won. There's nothing to be sorry about. You're a
winner. I'm the fuckin' loser. I should be sorry.

TRENT

Baby, don't talk like that, baby.

MIKE

Let's just leave.

TRENT

Baby, you're *money*. You're the *big* winner.

MIKE

Let's go.

TRENT
(condescending)
Who's the big winner?

Mike looks away, shaking his head in disgust.

TRENT
(lifting Mike's reluctant hand from the wrist like a boxing champ)
Mikey's the big winner.

MIKE
(shaking his head to hide a smirk)
What an asshole.

TRENT
Okay, Tee's the asshole, but Mikey's the big winner.

The same WAITRESS from before approaches the swingers as they are about to leave.

CHRISTY
There you two are. I walked around for an hour with that stupid scotch on my tray.

MIKE
Sorry. We got knocked out pretty quickly.

CHRISTY
(sarcasm?)
A couple of high rollers like you?

MIKE
Could you believe it?

CHRISTY
Wait here, I'll get you that scotch.

MIKE
Nah, I didn't really want it anyway. I just wanted to order it.

CHRISTY
Can I get you something else? I mean, you shouldn't leave without getting something for free.

MIKE
No thanks. Why ruin a perfect night?

TRENT
(condescending)

Bring a single malted Glengarry for me *and* my boy
Mikey, and if you tell the bartender to go easy on the
water . . .

(holds up a half-dollar)

. . . this Kennedy has your name on it. Now run along,
I'm timing you.

The waitress smiles in spite of herself, shakes her head, and walks away.

MIKE

What an asshole.

TRENT

That was *money*. Tell me that wasn't money.

MIKE

That was so demeaning . . .

TRENT

She *smiled*, baby.

MIKE

I can't believe what an asshole you are.

TRENT

Did she, or did she not smile?

MIKE

She was smiling at what an asshole you are.

TRENT

She was smiling at how *money* I am, baby.

MIKE

Let's go. I'm not paying for a room, and if we don't
leave now we'll never make it.

TRENT

Leave? The honey-baby's bringing us some cocktails.

MIKE

What are you, nuts? You think she's coming back?

TRENT

I *know* she's coming back.

MIKE

I don't think so.

TRENT

Baby, did you hear her? "You shouldn't leave without getting something for free." She wants to party, baby.

MIKE

You think so?

TRENT

You gotta give Tee one thing. He's good with the ladies.

MIKE

I'm too tired for this. Let's just go.

TRENT

Baby, this is what we came here for. We met a beautiful baby and she likes you.

MIKE

She likes *you*.

TRENT

Whatever. We'll see. Daddy's gonna get her to bring a friend. We'll both get one. I don't care if I'm with her or one of her beautiful baby friends.

MIKE

I don't know . . .

TRENT

You gotta get that girl out of your head. It's time to move on. You're a stylish, successful, good-looking cat. The ladies want to love you, you just gotta let them.

MIKE

That's bullshit.

TRENT

It's not. You're *money*. Any of these ladies would be
lucky to pull a cat like you.

MIKE

It's just that I've been out of the game so long. Trent, I
was with her for *six years*. That's before AIDS. I'm
scared. I don't know how to talk to them, I don't
know . . .

TRENT

You can't think like that, baby. It's hard, I know. I've
been there. Not for six years, but I know. You just gotta
get back out there.

MIKE

It's just tough, after sleeping with someone you love for
so long, to be with someone new . . . who doesn't
know what I like . . . and you *gotta* wear a jimmy . . .

TRENT

. . . *gotta* . . .

MIKE

. . . and then I'm struggling to maintain a conversation
with some chick who's not half as classy as my
girlfriend, who I'm not even attracted to . . .

TRENT

Oh, I don't even know what they're talking about half
the time. I can't keep track if they're talking about their
father who couldn't show affection or how hard it is to
be adopted. I just stare at their mouth and crinkle my
brow and they think I'm the sweetie. Now this girl
here, she's a waitress in Vegas, but I'll bet you anything
she's got a special dream and, no matter what I do, I'm
gonna hear all about it. And that's "one to grow
on . . ."

Tee turns his head just in time to greet the WAITRESS who, thank God, barely missed his comment.

> **TRENT**
> *(looking at watch)*
> . . . One fifty-nine, two minutes. And here she is. The most special girl in town.

> **CHRISTY**
> Two Glengarrys, down, easy on the water.

> **TRENT**
> Beautiful. What time are you off . . .
> *(reads nameplate)*
> . . . Christy?

> **CHRISTY**
> Six.

Mike can't believe it. Tee is just making it happen.

> **TRENT**
> Call a friend and have her meet the three of us at the Bamboo Lounge at six-*oh-one.*
> *(Trent throws the half-dollar on her tray)*
> And this is for you because you earned it.

CUT TO:
INT. CASINO—JUNGLE THEME COFFEE SHOP—SAME NIGHT

Trent and Mike are looking at menus. They're smoking at the table because they can.

> **MIKE**
> That was so fuckin' *money.* It was like that "Jedi mind" shit.

TRENT

That's what I'm telling you, baby. The babies love that
stuff. They don't want all that sensitive shit. You start
talking to them about puppy dogs and ice cream. They
know what you *want*. What do you think? You think
they don't know?

MIKE

I know. I know.

TRENT

They know what you want, believe me. Pretending is
just a waste of time. You're gonna take them there
eventually anyway. Don't apologize for it.

MIKE

I'm just trying to be a gentleman, show some
respect . . .

TRENT

Respect, my ass. They respect honesty. You see how
they dress when they go out? They want to be noticed.
You're just showing them it's working. You gotta get
off this respect kick, baby. There ain't nothing wrong
with letting them know that you're money and that
you want to party.

*The COFFEE SHOP WAITRESS approaches the table. She's cute, but
not nearly as hot as Christy.*

WAITRESS

Are you ready to order?

MIKE

Coffee . . .
            (points to Trent, who nods)
Two coffees. It says "Breakfast Any Time," right?

WAITRESS

That's right.

MIKE
I'll have pancakes in the "Age of Enlightenment."

It goes over like a lead balloon.

WAITRESS
And you?

TRENT
I'll have the Toucan over easy.

WAITRESS
I'll be back with the coffee.

She takes the menus and goes.

TRENT
(genuinely)
Nice, baby.

MIKE
I should've said Renaissance, right? It went over her head.

TRENT
Baby, you did fine.

MIKE
(disgusted with himself)
"Age of Enlightenment." Shit. Like some waitress in a Las Vegas coffee shop is going to get an obscure French philosophical reference. How demeaning.
I may as well have just said "Let me jump your ignorant bones."

TRENT
. . . Baby . . .

MIKE
. . . It's just, I thought "Renaissance" was too Excalibur, it's the wrong casino. She would've *gotten* it, though . . .

TRENT

You did fine. Don't sweat her. We're meeting *our*
honeys soon. You *know* Christy's friend is going to be
money.

MIKE

I hope so.
(checks watch)
We gotta go soon.

TRENT

Baby, relax. It's just down the hall. She's gotta change
. . . we'll be fine.

MIKE

We didn't do so bad after all.

TRENT

Baby, we're *money*.

*Mike tries to catch the attention of their waitress, who is passing with a huge
platter containing a BREAKFAST BANQUET.*

MIKE

Excuse me. We're in a bit of a hurry . . .

WAITRESS

Hang on, Voltaire.

*She passes their table and sets the ENTIRE FEAST in front of the
BLUEHAIR from the casino, who sits alone.*

BLUEHAIR

I said *two* lox platters. This isn't thirty dollars' worth of
food. I have a *thirty-dollar* voucher. This isn't my first
time in Vegas, you know.

CUT TO:
INT. CASINO—BAMBOO LOUNGE—
SAME NIGHT

Christy is at the bar wearing acid-washed jeans with a matching denim top. She's sexy in a pathetic mid-eighties sort of way. She's sitting next to a pretty brunette, LISA, dressed in a similar fashion.

There is something bizarre about her appearance. Her hair is tied into long pigtails with powder blue ribbons. Her makeup job is almost theatrical, with bright pink/red lips. She can't be that out of it, or can she?

The girls have already been flanked by a herd of potential COURTIERS.

The SWINGERS saunter up to the girls in a smooth, SLOW-MOTION SHOT.

The girls notice them.

The courtiers sense their rejection and part like the Red Sea for the swingers in perfect slow-motion choreography.

> **CHRISTY**
> Hi, boys, we almost gave up on you.

> **TRENT**
> Oh, are we late? There are no clocks in this town.

> **CHRISTY**
> Well, no harm done. This is Lisa. I'm sorry, I never got your names . . .

> **MIKE**
> I'm Mike . . .
> *(with contempt)*
> and this is my friend Doubledown Trent.

> **TRENT**
> *(working the bit)*
> Stop.
> *(then to the girls)*
> Ladies, don't you double down on an eleven?

CHRISTY

Always . . .

LISA

No matter *what* . . . like splitting aces.

MIKE

Whatever.

TRENT

Hello, Lisa. I'm Trent. What a lovely makeup job.

CHRISTY

Lisa works at the MGM Grand . . .

LISA
(apologetically)

I'm a "Dorothy."

TRENT
(trying to sell her to Mike)

Oh . . . a *Dorothy.*

MIKE

Well . . . we're not in Kansas anymore.

Another lead balloon. Uncomfortable silence.

CHRISTY

What do you guys do?

MIKE

I'm a comedian.

More uncomfortable silence.

LISA

Do you ever perform out here? I'd love to see you.

MIKE

No . . .

LISA

You should. A lot of comics play Vegas.

MIKE

Well, I'm afraid it's not that easy . . .

LISA

Why not?

MIKE

There are different circuits . . . it's hard to explain . . .
you wouldn't understand . . .

LISA

Who's your booking agent?

MIKE
(flustered)

Oh? You know about booking agents . . . I don't, uh,
actually have a *West Coast* agent as of yet . . .

LISA

Well, who represents you Back East?

MIKE

Actually, it's funny you . . . I'm actually, uh, *between* . . .

LISA

What do you do, Trent?

TRENT

I'm a producer.

BOTH GIRLS

Wow . . . Oooh . . . Ahhh . . .

Mike rolls his eyes at how full of shit Trent is.

CHRISTY

Listen, I'm not really allowed to drink here. We should
go someplace else. How's my place?

The swingers exchange a glance.

Beat.

> **TRENT AND MIKE**
> Sounds good to me . . . Fine . . . Sure.

CUT TO:
EXT. CHRISTY'S TRAILER—EARLY MORNING

Establishing shot of an Airstream trailer dug into the desert on chocks. Trent's car and two El Caminos are parked out front.

INT. CHRISTY'S TRAILER—SAME

The foursome, now somewhat more intimate, sit huddled around the fold-out table.

They've been drinking whiskey and long-neck Buds, judging by the recyclables.

The pairings seem to be Trent/Christy, Mike/Lisa.

The cramped compartment is filled with secondary smoke and laughter.

> **TRENT**
> No . . . no . . . The worst was when I went in for this after-school special and I'm sitting in the waiting room with all these little kids. I see they're all signed in for the same role as me . . .

> **CHRISTY**
> They were auditioning for the same role as you?

TRENT

Wait . . . Wait . . . Listen . . . So, I check the time and
place. I'm where I'm supposed to be. I call my agent
. . . She says they asked for me specifically . . .

MIKE

What was the part?

TRENT

Oh . . . "I love you . . . I can't believe you're doing
this . . . Drugs are bad . . ." Whatever. After-school
bullshit. The role is Brother.

MIKE

Big Brother, Little Brother?

TRENT

Wait . . . Wait . . . Just Brother. So I go in. "Hello . . .
Hi . . . We loved your guest spot on Baywatch . . . blah
blah blah . . ." Whatever. So, I start to read, and, Mikey,
I was money. I prepared for a week. It's a starring role.
I'm crying . . . The casting director, she starts crying . . .

MIKE

No!

TRENT

Yes!

LISA

Oh my God.

CHRISTY

Did you get it?

TRENT

Wait . . . She's crying. I finish. I hold up my finger like
"Wait a second." They sit in silence for, like, at least
five minutes. I look up and they all start *clapping*, and
now they're *all* crying. Even the *camera guy.*

MIKE

No! Not the camera guy!

TRENT

I'm telling you!

LISA

So, what happened?

TRENT

So, I swear to God this is exactly what he said. The
producer says to me . . . now he's still crying . . . he
says to me that I was great, that that was exactly what
they were looking for . . .

MIKE

. . . So give me the fuckin' part . . .

TRENT

Right? . . . that I nailed it . . . Whatever. Then he says
it's just that I'm a *little old*. I'm like "How old is the
Brother?". He's like, he says this with a straight face, I
swear to God, he says "*Eleven*."

MIKE

So, what'd you say to him? *Double down*?

They all crack up even more.

TRENT

It's like, you looked at my tape. You saw my picture.
Why did you call me in? You knew I was twenty-four.

CHRISTY

What an asshole.

MIKE

I believe it.

*The room dies down. The girls settle into the arms of their men. There's a lot
of body language and pheromones, but not a lot of words.*

CHRISTY

How rude of me. I haven't given you the tour.

She gets up and leads Trent into the sleeping compartment to the rear. The door slaps shut.

Mike and Lisa, in all her made-up glory, look into each other's eyes.

CUT TO:
INT. CHRISTY'S TRAILER—SLEEPING COMPARTMENT—SAME

Trent is already at work. He's smooth. A cascade of stuffed animals tumble off the bed with every thrust. Clothes start to peel off.

Trent takes a breather. He takes a step to the door.

TRENT

Let me just check on my boy.

CHRISTY

Don't worry. He's in good hands.

Trent cracks the door and peers through. The light is dim, but he can make out that they're starting to neck.

He closes the door, satisfied.

CHRISTY
(coyly)
What a good friend. I can use a friend like you.
(she beckons him back to bed)

CUT TO:
INT. CHRISTY'S TRAILER—FRONT ROOM—SAME

What seemed like necking is actually Lisa and Mike huddled tight having an intimate conversation.

LISA
(reassuring)
I'm sure she'll call. Six years is a long time. You don't just break it off cleanly after six years.

MIKE
I know, but she did. She's with someone else now . . .

LISA
Already? You poor thing. It won't last.

MIKE
Why not?

LISA
It's a rebound.

MIKE
We were a rebound, and we lasted for six years.

LISA
Yeah, but how long was the relationship she was rebounding *from*?

MIKE
Six years.

Beat.

MIKE
Can I check my messages? I have a calling card.

LISA
Sure, I guess. The phone's in the back.

Mike gets up and approaches the door.

MIKE
Sorry, it's just that . . .

LISA

I understand.

Mike lightly knocks on the door.

MIKE

Trent . . .
> *(knock knock)*

Tee.

The door cracks.

MIKE

Sorry, man. I need . . .

Trent pokes a CONDOM through the door.

MIKE

No, man. I need to use the phone.

TRENT

What?

MIKE

I gotta use the phone.

TRENT

Baby, you'll check them tomorrow.

MIKE

Please, Tee. I have to use the phone. Sorry, man.

TRENT

Hold on.

The door closes.

MIKE
> *(to Lisa)*

I hope I'm not interrupting anything. They weren't in there that long.

Lisa reassuringly shakes her head.

Beat.

Christy walks out wearing only Trent's sharkskin jacket as a robe.

Trent follows with a towel wrapped around his waist.

Trent glares at Mike as they pass. Daggers.

> ### MIKE
> *(apologizing to Christy as he exits)*
> I've got a calling card, there's no charge to your phone.

CUT TO:
INT. CHRISTY'S TRAILER—SLEEPING COMPARTMENT—SAME

Mike dials.

BACK TO:
INT. CHRISTY'S TRAILER—FRONT ROOM—SAME

Half-naked Trent and Christy sit with fully clothed Lisa.

> ### CHRISTY
> *(to Lisa)*
> The poor thing. Six years?

> ### LISA
> . . . And she's with someone else.

CHRISTY

The poor thing. I'll make some coffee.

Trent is not happy.

BACK TO:
INT. CHRISTY'S TRAILER—SLEEPING
COMPARTMENT—SAME

Mike is on the phone.

ANSWERING MACHINE
(synthesized voice)

She didn't call.

Disappointment pulls at Mike's brow.

BACK TO:
INT. CHRISTY'S TRAILER—FRONT
ROOM—SAME

The girls clean up the bottles and ashtrays. The coffee is brewing. The shades are up. It's officially morning.

Trent's chin is in his hand. He radiates the blue tinge of glandular congestion. He'll have no part of any of this.

CHRISTY

He's so sweet. He really said that?

LISA

I believe it too. He really just wants her to be happy.

CHRISTY

He is *so* sweet.

Mike enters.

The girls immediately stop their chatter and look to him in anticipation.

Mike shakes his head "no."

The girls walk to embrace him in consolation.

> **BOTH GIRLS**
> Awwww.

Trent just shakes his head. He'll have no part of any of this.

CUT TO:
EXT. DESERT ROAD—A DUSTY SHOULDER—NEVADA—DAY

Trent is in a LOOSE CLOSE-UP in the foreground. Mike leans out of the passenger seat in the background.

> **MIKE**
> She asked me what I was thinking about. What should
> I have done? Lie?

> **TRENT**
> You didn't have to get into it, baby.

> **MIKE**
> Sorry about interrupting . . .

> **TRENT**
> Don't worry about me, baby. I just wanted you to have
> a good time.

> **MIKE**
> Christy was nice . . .

Trent zips his fly and backs up, revealing that he was taking a long leak. Both he and Mike are half-dressed to Italian Ts and disheveled as shit.

TRENT

I didn't even like her, to be honest.

MIKE

She was hot.

TRENT

She didn't really do it for me, baby. How'd you like
Dorothy?

MIKE

I don't know. The whole Judy Garland thing kind of
turned me on. Does that make me some kind of fag?

TRENT

No, baby. You're money.

Trent starts the car.

MIKE

She didn't like me, anyway.

TRENT

She thought you were money.

MIKE

I don't think so.

TRENT

I heard them talking. They both thought you were
money.

MIKE

Yeah, a good friend.

Trent turns off the car and turns to face Mike.

TRENT

Baby, you take your*self* out of the game. You start
talking about puppy dogs and ice cream, of course it's
gonna be on the friend tip.

MIKE

I just don't think she liked me in that way.

TRENT

Baby, you're so money and you don't even know it.

MIKE

Tee, girls don't go for me the way they go for you.

TRENT

Michelle went for you, right?

MIKE

That was different.

TRENT

How?

MIKE

I was younger . . . It was college. You didn't go to college, you don't know what it's like. The girls are young, they don't know any better.

TRENT

That's just plain silly. Your self-esteem is just low because she's with someone else. But thinking about it and talking about it all the time is bad. It's no good, man. You gotta get out there. The ladies want to love you, baby.

MIKE

I just need some time . . .

TRENT

Why? So you can beat yourself up? Sitting around in that stuffy apartment. It's just plain bad for you, man. It's depressing. You've come so far. Remember the first week? After she told you? You couldn't even eat.

MIKE

Don't remind me.

TRENT

You just sat around drinking orange juice. Now look at
you. Look how far you've come in just a few months.
You got that part in that movie . . .

MIKE

. . . a *day* . . .

TRENT

. . . Whatever. It's work. You're doing what you love.
What's she doing?

MIKE

Selling scrap metal.

TRENT
(smiles)
See? And what does this guy she's with do?

MIKE

He drives a carriage.

TRENT

What?!?

MIKE
(smiling)
I hear he drives a carriage around Central Park or
something.

TRENT

Please. And you're sweating *him*? You're the party guy
and you're sweating some lawn jockey? Baby, she's the
one who should be thinking about *you*. Sounds to me
like you cut loose some dead weight. Trust me, Mikey,
you're better off.

Trent starts the car. Frank sings from the dashboard.

MIKE

I'm gonna try. I'm really gonna try.

The Comet pulls out onto the southbound I-15 leaving behind a swirl of dust.

EXT. DESERT ROAD—SAME

Trent's car drives off into the distance leaving behind a sign reading: LOS
ANGELES—270 MILES.

FADE TO:
EXT. PITCH AND PUTT GOLF
COURSE—LOS FELIZ—DAY I

Establishing shot of MIKE and ROB teeing off with nine irons.

*Rob wears a Yale sweatshirt. Mike wears one from Queens College. A Mets
cap shades his eyes. Neither have shaved and, odds are, neither showered.
They each carry a loose nine blade and putter as they wander to their lie.*

> **ROB**
> I don't think I'm gonna take it.

> **MIKE**
> It's a gig.

> **ROB**
> I mean, I need the money.

> **MIKE**
> You're an actor. Find the Zen in the role.

> **ROB**
> It's definitely a step back for me.

> **MIKE**
> Look, there's not much of a call for Shakespeare in this
> town.

> **ROB**
> There's just something about being Goofy. Any other
> Disney character would be fine. There's just this stigma
> associated with that character.

> **MIKE**
>
> What do you want? You're tall.

> **ROB**
>
> Do you realize how hard it's going to be to tell my parents? I still haven't told them I didn't get the pilot.

> **MIKE**
>
> You tested over a month ago. I'm sure they figured it out by now.

> **ROB**
>
> It's like "Hi, Mom. I'm not going to be starring in that sitcom and, oh by the way, I'm Goofy. Send more money."

They split up and both overchip the green miserably.

CUT TO:
EXT. PUTTING GREEN—PITCH AND PUTT GOLF COURSE—SAME

Mike and Rob putt.

> **MIKE**
>
> Haven't you noticed I didn't mention Michelle once today?

> **ROB**
>
> I didn't want to say anything.

> **MIKE**
>
> Why?

> **ROB**
>
> I don't know. It's like not talking to a pitcher in the midst of a no-hitter.

MIKE

What? Like, you didn't want to jinx it?

ROB

Kinda.

MIKE

I don't talk about her *that* much.

ROB

Oh no?

MIKE

I didn't mention her once today.

ROB

Well, until now. Tend the pin.

Mike pulls out the flag for Rob's putt. He misses.

MIKE

The only reason I mentioned her at all is to say that I'm not going to talk about her anymore. I thought you'd appreciate that.

ROB

I do. Good for you, man.

MIKE

I've decided to get out there.
(re: the ball)
Go ahead. Play it out.

Rob putts the "gimme." He misses by an inch.

MIKE

I'm not making any more excuses for myself.

Rob taps it in. He then tends the pin for Mike, who misses.

ROB

Good to hear, Mikey.

Mike putts again, and misses.

MIKE

You want to hit the town tonight?

ROB

I shouldn't, Mike, it's a weeknight.

MIKE

What do you have? A Pluto callback?

ROB

Sure. Kick me when I'm down.

Mike plunks it in.

MIKE

Count 'em up.

The two of them count and recount as they revisualize each shot in their head. Throughout this process they count under their breath and point to different parts of the fairway and green.

The two of them revolve, point, and mumble for an absurdly long amount of time until finally . . .

ROB

How many strokes?

MIKE

I don't know. Eight or nine.

ROB

I'll give you an eight.
                    (writes score)

MIKE

What'd you get?

ROB

An eight.

MIKE

Looks like we're in a dead heat after one hole. This is turning into quite a rivalry.

Rob points to the far-off crowd of a dozen IRATE GOLFERS waiting to tee off.

ROB

You better replace the pin, Chi-Chi. The natives look restless.

CUT TO:
INT. SUE'S APARTMENT—HOLLYWOOD BOULEVARD—EVENING

First of all, SUE is a guy, and a tough guy at that. He is wearing an L.A. Kings home jersey. His sweater bears the sacred number 99. His forearms are covered with tattoos of dice, playing cards, and a Varga girl. Sue is lounging in front of the TV in cuffed bluejeans and engineer boots. A heavy chain protects his empty wallet. Straight-up greaser.

Sue brushes back a shock of heavily greased black hair as not to obscure his view of the screen. His face glows with the reflection of the SEGA HOCKEY game on the set. Sue and TRENT are locked in a heavily contested battle of motor reflexes. Nothing moves but their eyes, thumbs, and mouths . . .

SUE

Bitch . . . You little bitch!

TRENT

Chelios to Roenick . . . !

The rockabilly twang of an electric Gretsch hollowbody blares over the stereo.

The room, like the guys, could use a spring cleaning. Pizza boxes, beer bottles, and full, full ashtrays. You can taste the smoke.

SUE

You little bitch!

MIKE

Hey Sue. Gretzky's on his ass again.

TRENT

Because he's a bitch.

SUE

That's so bullshit. This is so bullshit.

MIKE

You should play another team. The Kings are bitches in this game.

SUE

Hey, man. I took the Kings to the *Cup*.

TRENT

. . . against the *computer*.

SUE

They're a finesse team . . .

TRENT

They're a bitch team . . . *Score! Roenick!*

SUE

Fuck!!! That is so *bullshit*!

MIKE

Give it up, Sue.

The PHONE RINGS. Sue picks it up and balances it on his shoulder as he plays.

SUE

Hello?

(re: game)

Shit!
                    (back to phone)
Yeah. The elevator doesn't work.
                    (He lets the phone drop. Then to Mike)
It's Pink Dot. Buzz him in—hit nine.

*Mike picks the phone up off the matted shag carpet. He pushes 9, listens,
then hangs up.*

TRENT

I wish the game still had fights so I could bitch-slap
Wayne.

MIKE

This version doesn't have fighting?

TRENT

No. Doesn't that suck?

MIKE

Why? That was the best part of the old game.

SUE

I don't know. I guess kids were hitting each other or
something.

TRENT

You could make their heads bleed, though.

SUE

Yeah . . . If you hit them hard their heads bleed all over
the ice and their legs convulse.

MIKE

No.

TRENT

Yeah.

SUE

It's kinda money, actually.

MIKE

Make someone bleed.

SUE

No, man, we're in the play-offs.

TRENT

I'll make Gretzky bleed, the little bitch.

The DELIVERY MAN knocks on the door.

SUE

Pause it.

(Trent pauses the game.)

MIKE

Give me the money. I'll get it.

While Sue gives Mike the money, Trent UNPAUSES the game and checks Gretzky into the boards, leaving him writhing in a pool of red pixels.

SUE

You *bitch*!

Sue dives onto Trent. They wrestle a little too rambunctiously for indoors. Trent pulls the hockey sweater over Sue's head and starts wailing on his back.

Mike crosses. The CAMERA follows him down a shallow hallway to the door. He unlocks it.

A delivery man of eastern-hemispheric descent is out of breath from four flights of stairs. He hands Mike a twelve-pack of Bud cans and three packs of Marlboro reds.

He can HEAR, but NOT SEE, the chaos ensuing in the living room.

CUT TO:
INT. SUE'S LIVING ROOM—CONTINUOUS

Trent and Sue are flushed. They pause long enough to torment Mike.

TRENT
(feigning homosexuality)
Is he *cute*? Ask him if he wants to stay for a cocktail!

SUE
(following suit)
. . . Is he *brown*?

BACK TO:
INT. SUE'S DOORWAY—CONTINUOUS

Mike forces an apologetic smile. He is embarrassed. The delivery man doesn't seem to understand any of this.

Mike, out of guilt, hands him a four-dollar tip. This he seems to understand. He smiles and leaves.

Mike crosses back to the main room.

MIKE
You guys are such assholes.

TRENT
(continuing the gag)
Aww . . . He got away?

SUE
(untangling himself from Trent)
Gimme my reds. I've been jonesing for an hour.

Mike throws him a pack of smokes, which he unravels with surgical precision.

Cans of beer are tossed around and cracked.

MIKE
What time's this party tonight?

TRENT
It starts at eight . . .

SUE

. . . which means no one will get there till ten.

MIKE

So, what? Eleven?

TRENT AND SUE

Midnight.

MIKE

I'm gonna bring an old friend who just moved out here.

TRENT

Who? Rob?

MIKE

Yeah. You met him once.

TRENT
(approvingly)
Yeah. He's a rounder.

SUE

What's he do?

MIKE

He's trying to be an actor.

TRENT

What a surprise . . .

SUE

. . . How novel.

CUT TO:
**EXT. DARK ALLEY—OFF OF HOLLYWOOD
BLVD.—SEEDY—NIGHT**

*MIKE and ROB walk down the dirty deserted alleyway. Mike is wearing
baggy slacks and an oversized Eisenhower-cut jacket with a vertical stripe*

inset. The collar is large and pointy, but definitely not seventies. His ensemble has more of an early sixties vibe.

Rob hasn't been at it quite as long, but still manages to qualify as ''the lounge guy.''

Mike walks with purpose. He intermittently tries to pull open locked steel doors along the alley. Rob looks confused.

> ### ROB
>
> So, if the party starts at eight, why are we first going to a bar at ten?

> ### MIKE
>
> To get a drink before we meet the guys for a bite at eleven.

> ### ROB
>
> Oh.
>> *(beat)*
>
> Where is this place?

> ### MIKE
>> *(pulling a handle)*
>
> It's one of these. For some reason, cool bars in L.A. have to be very hard to find and have no signs out front.

> ### ROB
>
> That doesn't sound too good for business.

> ### MIKE
>> *(pull)*
>
> It's kinda like a speakeasy kind of thing. It's kinda cool. It's like you're in on some kind of secret. You tell a chick you've been someplace, it's like bragging that you know how to find it. Now, as time goes on, more people know how to find it and it gradually becomes less and less cool. A Hollywood nightclub has a half-life of about three months, then it starts to fade. Now this place here just opened, so you have to be very selective about who you bring with you.

>   **ROB**
> Should I be blindfolded?

>   **MIKE**
> Don't laugh. I heard they cut the tongues out of the
> people who built it.

*At this point they come upon an unmarked BLACK METAL DOOR,
which Mike successfully pulls open to reveal . . .*

.

INT. HOLLYWOOD CLUB—SAME

*A smoke-filled, windowless, black-walled room. There are several round
padded booths lining the walls. The place is packed, and the funk standard
"Brick House" throbs over the P.A.*

*A HANDHELD SHOT as the two guys serpentine to the mirrored bar at
the far end of the room. Enshrined in its center is a framed photograph of
SINATRA smiling in approval as he presides over the evening's activities.*

Mike proudly points out the photo to Rob.

>   **MIKE**
> Kinda money, huh?

>   **ROB**
>   *(smiling)*
> Classy.

Mike catches the attention of a sexy female BARTENDER.

>   **MIKE**
> I'll get a Dewars rocks . . .
>   *(looks to Rob)*

>   **ROB**
> Bud.

MIKE

. . . A Dewars on the rocks and a Bud, please.

She goes.

ROB

I can't get over how cute the girls in this city are.

MIKE

I know. It's like the opposite of inbreeding. The hottest
one percent from around the world migrate to this gene
pool.

ROB

Darwinism at its best.

MIKE

I've been here six months and I still can't get over it.

ROB

It's like, *every day* I see a beautiful woman. I'm not used
to that. I'm used to seeing a beautiful woman, I don't
know, once a week. I can't handle it.

MIKE

Wait till summer. I swear, you can't leave the house. It
hurts. It physically hurts.

ROB

I can't wait till I actually get to touch one of them.

MIKE

Ah, there's the rub . . .

ROB

There's the rub.

The bartender serves them their drinks.

CHARLES
(offscreen)

Whassup, Mikey?

Mike turns to see CHARLES. A young black man with a tight Dolomite fro. He wears a black leather blazer over a black turtleneck. The coolest guy in three counties.

A handshake turns into a hug.

MIKE
Charles! What's up, man?

CHARLES
Oh. You know.

MIKE
Did you, um, did you get that pilot?

CHARLES
No, man. I know you didn't get it 'cause you wouldn't't've asked me. It wasn't that funny anyway . . .

MIKE
. . . piece of shit. Listen, Charles, this is my friend Rob from Back East.

Shake.

CHARLES
Hi.

ROB
My pleasure.

MIKE
Charles and me went to network on this pilot together.

ROB
I just tested for one . . .

MIKE
. . . yeah, a month ago.

CHARLES
Oh, I'm sorry. How'd your folks take it?

ROB

I haven't heard an official "no" yet.

CHARLES

You haven't told them, huh?

ROB

No.

CHARLES

I still haven't told my folks I didn't get *Deep Space 9*.
You'd think they'd'a figured it out by now, but Mom
keeps asking . . .

MIKE

. . . and boy does it hurt when they ask.

CHARLES

I don't even tell them about anything I'm close on
anymore . . .

MIKE

. . . not until you book it . . .

CHARLES

. . . and even then . . .

MIKE

. . . you might get cut out.

ROB

I'm considering taking a job as a Goofy.

CHARLES

Hey, man. At least it's Disney.

MIKE

You want to come with us to a party at the Chateau
Marmont? They got a bungalow and lots of beautiful
babies.

CHARLES
(yelling over the roar of the wall-to-wall crowd)
Why not? This place is dead anyway.

CUT TO:
INT. HOLLYWOOD HILLS
DINER—FRANKLIN AVE.—LATER THAT
NIGHT

MIKE, TRENT, SUE, CHARLES, and ROB sit around a table. All of our boys are classily dressed. They wear a lot of black, brown, and gray with a splash of gold and maroon. There's enough shit in their hair to lube a Humvee.

The CAMERA REVOLVES around the table in a repeating Reservoir Dogs–*style over the shoulder 360-DEGREE PAN.*

TRENT
. . . No, baby. I got a better one. You gotta admit that the steadycam shot in *Goodfellas* was the money . . .

ROB
. . . through the basement of that restaurant . . .

MIKE
. . . the Copa, in New York . . .

TRENT
. . . through the kitchen . . .

CHARLES
. . . I heard it took four days to light for that shot . . .

ROB
. . . Four days . . . ?

SUE
. . . I don't know about *four* days . . .

CHARLES
. . . That's what I heard . . .

MIKE
. . . Maybe. I mean you gotta hide all the lights . . .

ROB
. . . That's got to cost a fortune . . .

CHARLES
. . . That's nothing, shit. You know how much he blew on his Vegas movie . . . ?

MIKE
. . . You gotta be nuts to shoot in a real casino . . .

TRENT
. . . *Mean Streets* was the bomb.

SUE
. . . Dude, *Reservoir Dogs*. With that shot . . .

ROB
. . . Which one?

SUE
. . . In the beginning. When they're walking in slow motion . . .

MIKE
. . . How can you compare them? Tarantino totally bites everything from Scorsese . . .

SUE
. . . He's *derivative* . . .

TRENT
. . . You gotta admit, it looked money . . .

CHARLES
. . . I heard they made that whole movie for *ten grand* . . .

ROB

. . . What's the big deal? Everyone steals from everyone.

MIKE
(checking his watch)
Well, let's hit that party.

CUT TO:
**EXT. SUNSET BOULEVARD—HEADLIGHTS
AND NEON—NIGHT**

*The five swingers walk down the boulevard in a SLO-MO SHOT which is
extremely derivative of the* Reservoir Dogs *credit sequence.*

*The scene is choreographed to Bennett's big band arrangement of "O SOLE
MIO."*

CUT TO:
**EXT. CHATEAU MARMONT
BUNGALOW—OUTSIDE THE
PARTY—MIDNIGHT**

*Muffled music seeps through the door. The swingers turn the knob and
enter . . .*

**INT. THE PARTY—CHATEAU MARMONT
BUNGALOW—SAME**

*The huge sunken living room is packed with people congealed into circles of
conversation and sipping cocktails.*

*EVERYTHING STOPS when they enter. The music, the conversations,
all movement, everything.*

Everyone in the room STARES at them standing in the doorway.

Beat.

The music starts back up and everyone returns to their conversations.

The CAMERA PANS across a row of a dozen trendy girls.
They all wear the same backpack.

The swingers weave their way through the crowd to . . .

INT. THE BAR AREA—THE BUNGALOW KITCHEN—SAME

The swingers fix themselves drinks from an assortment of bottles cluttering the table. They shamelessly paw at the top-shelf brands.

> **MIKE**
> Who threw this party, anyway?

> **SUE**
> Damned if I know . . .

> **TRENT**
> . . . Beats me . . .

> **CHARLES**
> . . . I came with *you.*

With that, the three of them peel off to work the room.

> **ROB**
> What's that guy's name? *Sue?*

> **MIKE**
> *Sue.* His dad was a big Johnny Cash fan.

> **ROB**
> Oh, like that song . . .

MIKE

. . . "A Boy Named Sue." I think that's why he's such a bad cat.

ROB

Him?

MIKE

He's a mean dude. I've seen him smash a guy's face into the curb. He knocked out his teeth . . . blood . . . He was just like boom, boom, boom . . . fuckin' nasty shit, man. He's a nice guy, though.

CUT TO:
INT. LIVING ROOM—BUNGALOW—SAME

Trent and Sue are scouting some LADIES across the room. One wears a short, sexy summer dress, combat boots, and is smoking a CIGAR. Intermittent eye contact has been established.

TRENT

Oh, it's *on*, baby . . .

SUE

. . . It's *on*.

BACK TO:
INT. LIVING ROOM—BUNGALOW—SAME

Mike and Rob have come back into the room. They scout the terrain.

MIKE

There are so many beautiful women here.

ROB

It's unbelievable.

MIKE

I got to at least try once.

ROB

You're a better man than I am, Charlie Brown.

MIKE

No, I just promised myself I'd give it a try. I gotta get
out there sooner or later.

ROB

Go for it, man.

*Mike spots a pair of beautiful BLONDES in black. They're wearing stretch
bell-bottoms and tops that expose their midriffs. The seventies never looked so
good.*

MIKE
(indicates the ladies)
I'm going in. Will you be my wingman?

ROB

I'll be your winger.

*They make the approach. With a great deal of effort, Mike catches their
attention . . .*

MIKE

Good evening, ladies—

Mike is interrupted by the party STOPPING to check another entrance.

Beat.

*The party RESUMES and the blondes redirect their attention to Mike. He
is a little put off but, God love him, he gets back in there.*

MIKE

How are you ladies doing this evening?

BLONDE

What do you drive?

MIKE

I'm sorry?

BLONDE

What kind of *car* do you drive?

MIKE

Oh . . . a Cavalier.

The blondes immediately enter back into their conversation as if they were never approached.

Mike and Rob exchange defeated glances.

One more try.

MIKE

. . . It's red?

CUT TO:
INT. LIVING ROOM—BUNGALOW—CONTINUOUS

Trent and Sue are trying to look like they're not paying attention to the group of ladies they saw across the room.

TRENT

Is she looking at me, baby?

SUE

No.

TRENT

Now?

SUE

No.

TRENT

Is she looking now?

SUE

No! She's not looking at you. She hasn't looked at you
once. Will you stop asking if . . . Wait, she just looked.

TRENT

See, baby?

Mike and Rob walk up to Trent and Sue.

MIKE

How you guys doing?

TRENT

It's on.

MIKE

Which one?

TRENT
(indicates the group of girls with a subtle head move)
Groucho.

*Mike and Rob STARE DIRECTLY at the girls like a deer in the headlights
. . . a big no-no.*

MIKE

The one with the cigar? She's cute.

Trent and Sue react with frustrated disappointment.

TRENT

What are you doing?

MIKE

What?

TRENT

You looked *right at* her, baby.

MIKE

She didn't notice.

> **SUE**
>
> Yes she did.

> **TRENT**
>
> Damn. Now I gotta go in early.

> **MIKE**
>
> I'm sorry.

> **TRENT**
>
> Don't sweat it, baby. This ones a layup.

Trent crosses away.

> **SUE**
>
> How's it going for you two?

> **MIKE**
>
> Not well.

> **SUE**
>
> Rejected?

> **ROB**
>
> Shaqed.

Mike's P.O.V. of Trent passing near and the GIRL WITH CIGAR. He says something, smiles, and points to her cigar. She laughs.

> **SUE**
>
> Well, just watch the T-bone and learn.

CUT TO:
INT. LIVING ROOM—TRENT'S
CONVERSATION—CONTINUOUS

Trent is having a sensitive one-on-one with the girl with the cigar.

GIRL WITH CIGAR
. . . I've always wanted to be an actress, at least as long
as I could remember. I went to . . .

*Under Trent's affirmative response we hear the first haunting TUBA PULSE
of the JAWS THEME:*

TRENT
(nodding in agreement)
Uhhhh . . . Huuuhhh.

CUT TO:

*CLOSE-UP of MIKE'S FACE as he looks on in HORRIFIED AWE
from afar.*

BACK TO:
INT. LIVING ROOM—TRENT'S
CONVERSATION—CONTINUOUS

GIRL WITH CIGAR
. . . Then one day after class my drama teacher, the one
who directed the play, said he thought I should . . .

The second TUBA PULSE accompanies Trent's sound of agreement:

TRENT
Uhhh . . . Huuhh.

BACK TO:
EXTREME CLOSE UP of MIKE's
HORRIFIED EYES

BACK TO:
INT. LIVING ROOM—TRENT'S
CONVERSATION—CONTINUOUS

GIRL WITH CIGAR
. . . I met with an agent last week, and I'm waiting to
hear . . .

The third, and progressively faster, TUBA PULSE sounds under Trent's response as the JAWS THEME begins to speed up and fill out:

TRENT
Uh-huh, Uh-huh, Uh-huh, Uh-huh . . . .

CUT TO:

Mike, Rob, and Sue look on.

SUE
Here comes the kill . . .

MATCH CUT TO:

The group's P.O.V. of the conversation.

The JAWS THEME reaches its violent crescendo as the girl looks into her purse.

Trent winks to the boys. Smooth.

She comes up with a pen and writes out her phone number.

Trent crosses back as the music dies away.

Using his body as a shield so the girl can't see, but so his boys can, he rips up and drops the number as he approaches them.

TRENT

Was I money?

MIKE

I don't know. It was kind of a dick move if you ask me.

TRENT

Why, baby? What'd I do wrong?

MIKE

You asked her for her number, and then you tore it up.

TRENT

She didn't see.

MIKE

That doesn't matter.

SUE

That *was* pretty cold, dude.

TRENT

What was cold about it?

The door opens. The party PAUSES to look, then RESUMES.

TRENT

She offered me her number. What should I have said?
"No?" *That* would've hurt her feelings. This way she
feels like the winner.

*Trent smiles and waves to her across the room. She coyly waves back and
makes the "phone sign" with her hand. Trent nods and smiles.*

TRENT

Tee can't roll with that, she's "business class."

ROB

"Business class?"

SUE
(explaining to Rob)
Big butt . . . you know, can't fly coach.

MIKE
I can't believe you.

Charles approaches the crew.

CHARLES
They're out of Glenlivet.

MIKE
What else is going on?

TRENT
We could hit the Dresden.

Overhead LONG SHOT of the swingers entrenched in the CROWDED PARTY.

SUE
Yeah. This place is dead, anyway.

CUT TO:
EXT. SUNSET BOULEVARD—OUTSIDE THE CHATEAU MARMONT—NIGHT

The swingers have left the party and are heading to their cars. They are all parked in a row, one behind the other. They each climb behind the wheel of their own car. They pull out in UNISON.

They travel like a train with their bumpers ALMOST TOUCHING.

CUT TO:
EXT. HOLLYWOOD STREETS—NIGHT

SHOTS of the CAR-TRAIN driving and making turns.

"O SOLE MIO" reprise.

DISSOLVE TO:
EXT. THE DRESDEN—VERMONT
AVE.—HOLLYWOOD—NIGHT

The car-train BREAKS UP to nose-in park behind the bar. They all "club"
their steering wheels.

CUT TO:
INT. THE DRESDEN—SAME

The SWINGERS lounge in a booth against the cork-paneled wall, sipping
cocktails. They watch MARTY and ELAYNE, the resident lounge act,
perform a jazz fusion cover of "Staying Alive" on synth and upright bass.
Marty greets Trent over the mike.

The room is busy, but not packed.

The swingers have all had a few.

>   **CHARLES**
>   I know what you're saying, man. I don't know what to
>   tell you . . .

>   **ROB**
>   . . . I mean, does it have to be *Goofy*? I was playing
>   Hamlet off Broadway two months ago, for crying out
>   loud . . .

Trent and Sue are involved in a different conversation. They are observing two HOT GIRLS at another cocktail table.

The girls are wearing short plaid skirts with black stockings pulled up to mid-thigh. It's the "catholic-school-girl-gone-bad" look.

The girls are a little too touchy-feely with each other, suggesting a certain sexual open-mindedness.

> **TRENT**
>
> It's *on*.

> **SUE**
>
> You think?

> **TRENT**
>
> Baby, I know it is. It's a black diamond trail . . .

> **SUE**
>
> . . . double diamond . . .

> **TRENT**
>
> . . . but it's worth the risk. True or false: It's worth the risk.

> **SUE**
>
> True.

As they get up to leave . . .

> **MIKE**
>
> God bless you guys.

They cross to the ladies.

Mike's P.O.V.

The girls seem at first cold, then receptive. Trent and Sue join their table and share some laughs.

Mike halfheartedly looks on. He is obviously not happy with where he stands on the bell curve of masculinity.

Mike, looking for any kind of escape, crosses to the bar.

CUT TO:
INT. BAR—DRESDEN ROOM—SAME

Mike unsuccessfully tries to catch the attention of the middle-aged BARTENDER.

> **MIKE**
> *(to himself)*
> I can't even get *this guy* to notice me . . .

A cute BLONDE (NIKKI) in a baby T and plastic mini chuckles at his comment from the bar.

Mike is at first self-conscious, then pushes ahead.

> **MIKE**
> You like laughing at the misery of others?

> **NIKKI**
> I'm sorry, I couldn't help it. Let me make it up to you.

She raises her finger and the bartender immediately approaches.

> **BARTENDER**
> What can I get you?

> **MIKE**
> I'll have a Dewars on the rocks.

He goes to fix it.

> **MIKE**
> Thanks.

NIKKI

I've seen you somewhere . . . Where have I seen you?

MIKE

You ever go to the Ha Ha Hole? On Pico?

NIKKI

. . . maybe . . .

MIKE

. . . Monday nights? I host an open mike . . .

NIKKI

You're a comedian?

MIKE

Yeah.

NIKKI

What's that like?

MIKE

(trying to bluff, not an ounce of sarcasm)

Well, you know, it's tough. A lot of traveling. A lot of
hotels . . . but, you know, it's a dream . . . and the
money's really good. I think I might buy another really
expensive imported car after my next gig in Vegas . . .

NIKKI

(politely interrupting)

I know! Starbucks! I served you an espresso at
Starbucks.

MIKE

Are you sure? Maybe . . .

NIKKI

Yes! Remember? You asked me for an application? I
introduced you to the manager?

MIKE
(trying to pull out of the dive)
Oh, yeah . . . Boy, that must've been a while ago.

NIKKI
I'd say about two weeks.

MIKE
Probably a little longer than that, but, whatever.

NIKKI
(smiling at him)
You better pay the man.

Mike notices the bartender, who has been waiting patiently with the drink.

MIKE
(fumbling with the money)
Oh . . . Sorry.

She chuckles. He pays and throws down a two-dollar tip apologetically.

MIKE
(tactical retreat)
Well, thank you . . . ?

NIKKI
Nikki.

MIKE
Thank you, Nikki.

He walks away kicking himself. He is intercepted by Trent and Sue, who both hold up cocktail napkins with scribbles.

TRENT
We got the digits, baby.

MIKE
What a surprise.

TRENT

What's wrong? I saw you talking to that beautiful blonde baby.

SUE

She was cute.

MIKE

She didn't like me . . . I made a fool of myself . . .

TRENT

Baby, don't talk that way, baby . . .

SUE

You are so money, and you don't even know it . . .

TRENT

That's what I keep trying to tell him.
(to Mike)
You're so money, you don't even know . . .

MIKE

Please, don't mess with me right now . . .

TRENT

We're not messing with you . . .

SUE

. . . we're not . . .

TRENT

You're like this big bear with claws and fangs . . .

SUE

. . . and big fuckin' teeth . . .

TRENT

. . . and teeth . . . And she's like this little bunny cowering in the corner . . .

SUE

. . . shivering . . .

TRENT

. . . And you're just looking at your claws like "How
do I kill this bunny"? . . .

SUE

. . . You're just poking at it . . .

TRENT

. . . Yeah. You're just gently batting it around . . . and
the rabbit's all scared . . .

SUE

. . . and you got big claws and fangs . . .

TRENT

. . . and fangs . . . and you're like "I don't know what
to do. How do I kill this bunny? . . ."

SUE

. . . you're like a big bear.

Beat. Mike smiles.

MIKE

You're not just, like, fucking with me?

TRENT

No, baby!

SUE

. . . honestly . . .

TRENT

. . . you're *money* . . .

SUE

. . . you're so fuckin *mmmoney*.

TRENT

Now go over there and get those digits.

SUE

You're money.

TRENT
(pulling him aside, dead serious)
Now when you talk to her, I don't want you to be the
guy in the PG–13 movie that everyone's pulling for. I
want you to be the guy in the rated R movie who
you're not sure if you like yet.

Mike nods and, energized by the bombardment, crosses back to the bar and right into the fray.

Trent and Sue rejoin the other swingers.

They all watch Mike operate.

Swingers' P.O.V. of Mike decisively engaging her in conversation.

She laughs.

Out comes the pen and the cocktail napkin. Bingo.

Mike crosses back to the swingers' table and, using his body to shield Nikki's view, pretends to rip the napkin. This breaks the guys up.

Mike sits down and, after admiring the blotchy numerals, delicately folds the napkin and pockets it.

TRENT

See, baby. It's not that hard.

CHARLES

Eight-one-eight?

MIKE

Three-one-oh.

Everyone reacts favorably to this area code.

MIKE

How long do I wait to call?

TRENT

A day.

MIKE

Tomorrow?

TRENT

No . . .

SUE

. . . Tomorrow, *then* a day.

TRENT

. . . Yeah.

MIKE

So, two days?

TRENT

Yeah. I guess you could call it that.

SUE

Definitely. Two days. That's the industry standard . . .

TRENT
(to Sue, shop talk)

. . . I used to wait two days. Now everyone waits two days. Three days is kinda the money now, don't you think?

SUE

. . . Yeah. But two's enough not to look anxious . . .

TRENT

Yeah, but three days is kinda the money . . .

MIKE
(interrupting sarcastically)

Why don't I just wait three weeks and tell her I was cleaning out my wallet and found her number . . .

CHARLES
. . . then ask where you met her . . .

MIKE
Yeah, I'll tell her I don't remember and then I'll ask
what she looks like.
(pause)
Then I'll ask if we fucked. How's that, Tee? Is that the
money?

The guys laugh.

TRENT
Laugh all you want, but if you call too soon you can
scare off a nice baby who's ready to party.

SUE
Don't listen to him. You call whenever it feels right to
you.

MIKE
How long are you guys gonna wait to call your honeys?

TRENT AND SUE
Six days.

CUT TO:
EXT. THE DRESDEN—PARKING LOT—OUT
BACK—NIGHT

*The swingers are leaving through the back door. The doorway is congested
with another group of guys who are entering.*

A BALD GUY with a goatee brushes by Sue.

SUE
Watch where you're going, asshole.

BALD GUY

What'd you say, bitch?

SUE

I said watch where you're going, bitch!

That's it. Now they're squaring off in the empty parking lot.

All the bald guy's boys fall in behind him. All the swingers fall in behind Sue. The swingers are not happy with Sue at all.

The two cliques contrast each other in every way.

The bald guys all have facial hair and multiple pierced extremities with the odd neck tattoo thrown in for good measure.

Baggy denim and boots. Pot leaves and Pumas. Long, heavy key chains. Vintage 1994 whiteboy faux-gangsta. They do, however, look big and mean next to our boys.

The early sixties-style sweater jackets and blazers over button-down shirts and tapered slacks don't quite have the same fear factor, but the boys do look classy.

The word "bitch" is growled out by the two of them a half dozen more times until . . .

Sue pulls a PISTOL out of his belt.

Everyone is SCARED. Especially the swingers.

SUE

Now what, bitch? Now who's the bitch, bitch?

The bald guys HOLD UP THEIR HANDS and slowly back up to their ride.

BALD GUY

Hey, man. I'm the bitch. I'm *your* bitch, okay? We're just gonna leave. Okay? I'm the bitch. I'm such a bitch, I can't even begin to tell you . . .

They jump in the car and SPEED AWAY.

Sue belts the gun and stands tall like Clint.

> **TRENT**
> What the fuck . . . ?

> **MIKE**
> What an asshole. Didn't you see *Boyz N the Hood*? Now
> one of *us* is gonna get shot.

> **SUE**
> He's a bitch. He ain't gonna do nothing.

> **MIKE**
> You asshole.

> **TRENT**
> You dick.

> **SUE**
> What'd you want me to do? Back down? He called me
> a bitch. We kept our rep, bro.

> **CHARLES**
> Fuck rep, I've got a callback tomorrow.

Charles leaves.

> **ROB**
> Yeah, I gotta be up early tomorrow.

Rob leaves, shaken up.

> **MIKE**
> You asshole. Why are you carrying a gun? What? In
> case someone steps to you, Snoop Dog?

> **SUE**
> Hey, man, you're not *from* here. You don't know how
> it is. I *grew up* in L.A. . . . .

TRENT

. . . Anaheim . . .

SUE

. . . Whatever. Things are different here. It's not like
New York, Mikey.

MIKE

Yeah. Here it's easier to avoid trouble. It's not like you
live in Compton where bullets are whizzing by your
head every day. Nobody's mugging you on no subway.
In New York the trouble finds you. Out here you gotta
go look for it . . .

SUE

. . . People get carjacked . . .

TRENT

. . . Oh, who would jack your fuckin K-car? He's right,
Sue. You don't need no gat.

SUE

Listen. Just because I was the only one with the balls to
stand up to them . . .

TRENT

. . . Oh yeah, like House of Pain was gonna *do*
anything . . .

MIKE

You live in such a fantasy world . . .

SUE

What about you, Mikey? At least I got balls. You're
always whining about some bitch who dumped you a
year ago . . .

MIKE

. . . It was six months, and she didn't dump . . .

SUE

. . . Whatever. You're like a whining little woman. Big

deal. You got a fuckin' number. Whoopee! You'll fuck
it up . . .

TRENT

. . . Sue . . .

SUE

Have you gotten laid *once* since you moved here? Did
you fuck once?

TRENT

. . . Shut up, Sue . . .

SUE

I know for a fact you haven't, because you never shut
up about it. You're like a little whiney bitch . . .

TRENT

Sue!

MIKE

No, Trent. He's right.

Mike walks to his car.

TRENT

Mikey!

Its too late. He's leaving.

Sue starts to open his mouth.

TRENT

Don't even talk to me.
                    (pause)
You *asshole.*

CUT TO:
INT. MIKE'S APARTMENT—LATER THAT NIGHT

Mike opens the door and flicks on the lights in his sparsely furnished single.

He drops his keys on the table and makes a beeline to the answering machine.

He pushes the button.

ANSWERING MACHINE
(synthesized voice)
She didn't call.

Mike collapses into his futon and lights a smoke.

Beat.

He pulls out the COCKTAIL NAPKIN. He stares at the number.

He looks at the clock. 2:20 A.M.

He looks at the napkin.

He thinks better of it, and puts the napkin away.

Beat.

He takes out the napkin and picks up the phone.

ANSWERING MACHINE
(synthesized voice)
Don't do it, Mike.

MIKE
Shut up.

He dials.

It rings twice, then . . .

NIKKI
(recorded)
Hi. This is Nikki. Leave a message.
(beep)

MIKE
Hi, Nikki. This is Mike. I met you tonight at the

Dresden. I, uh, just called to say I, uh, I'm really glad
we met and you should give me a call. So call me
tomorrow, or, like, in two days, whatever. My number
is 213–555–4679 . . .

(beep)

Mike hangs up.

Beat.

He dials again.

NIKKI
(recorded)
Hi. This is Nikki. Leave a message.
(beep)

MIKE
Hi, Nikki. This is Mike, again. I just called because it
sounded like your machine might've cut me off before
I gave you my number, and also to say sorry for calling
so late, but you were still there when I left the Dresden,
so I knew I'd get your machine. Anyway, my number
is . . .

(beep)

Mike calls back right away.

NIKKI
(recorded)
Hi. This is Nikki. Leave a message.
(beep)

MIKE
213–555–4679. That's all. I just wanted to leave my
number. I don't want you to think I'm weird, or
desperate or something . . .
(he regrets saying it immediately)
. . . I mean, you know, we should just hang out. That's
it. No expectations. Just, you know, hang out. Bye.
(beep)

He hangs up.

Beat.

He dials.

NIKKI
(recorded)
Hi. This is Nikki. Leave a message.
(beep)

MIKE

I just got out of a six-year relationship. Okay? That should help explain why I'm acting so weird. It's not you. It's me. I just wanted to say that. Sorry.
(pause)
This is Mike.
(beep)

He dials again. There's no turning back.

NIKKI
(recorded)
Hi. This is Nikki. Leave a message.
(beep)

MIKE

Hi, Nikki. This is Mike again. Could you just call me when you get in? I'll be up for a while, and I'd just rather talk to you in person instead of trying to squeeze it all . . .
(beep)

He dials yet again.

NIKKI
(recorded)
Hi. This is Nikki. Leave a message.
(beep)

MIKE

Hi, Nikki. Mike. I don't think this is working out. I

think you're great, but maybe we should just take some
time off from each other. It's not you, really. It's me.
It's only been six months . . .

NIKKI
(Live, in person. She picks up the line.)
Mike?

MIKE
Nikki! Great! Did you just walk in, or were you
listening all along?

NIKKI
(calmly)
Don't call me ever again.

MIKE
Wow, I guess you were home . . .
(click)

She hung up on him.

He's frozen.

He hangs up.

Beat.

Beat.

Beat.

FADE TO:
INT. MIKE'S APARTMENT—DAY

SHOT of answering machine.

ANSWERING MACHINE
(Trent's voice)
. . . Pick up . . . Pick up, Mikey . . . Are you home?

He is.

He is sitting in the middle of the floor under a comforter with a two-day beard. The miniblinds are sealed tight. He is surrounded by pictures, greeting cards, trinkets, full ashtrays, and empty Tropicana containers. Mike ignores the answering machine as he solemnly considers each of the items around him. He stares at a strip of four black-and-white arcade photos. They show he and MICHELLE hugging, kissing, and enjoying life.

> **ANSWERING MACHINE**
> *(Trent's voice)*
> . . . I guess you're not home. Why don't you come out tonight, baby. We haven't seen you for two days. We're gonna play hockey at Sue's house till ten-thirty, then we're either going to the Lava Lounge for Sinatra night, or the Derby for the Big Bad Voodoo Daddy. We might also check out Swing Night at the Viper. If we're not there we'll be at the Good Luck. Otherwise we'll be at the Three of Clubs. So come meet up with us. We'll see you there, gorgeous.
> *(beep)*

DISSOLVE TO:
INT. MIKE'S APARTMENT—NIGHT

He hasn't moved.

The PHONE RINGS.

He looks to the answering machine hopefully as it picks up after one ring.

> **ANSWERING MACHINE**
> *(Rob's voice)*
> Mikey . . . ? It's Rob. Pick up, buddy.

His shoulders slack with DISAPPOINTMENT. It's not her.

ANSWERING MACHINE
(Rob's voice)

... I'm downstairs. Buzz me in. I know you're home.
Your lights are on and your car's here. Come on,
buddy. Open up . . .

Mike puts down a Boynton card and picks up the phone. He pushes 9, and hangs up.

He lights a cigarette.

A knock at the door.

Mike opens it, and Rob walks in with a brown bag.

He surveys the scene. He's seen this before. He moves some laundry off an armchair and sits down.

He pulls a pepperoni and a loaf of semolina out of the bag.

He hands Mike a pint of orange juice.

MIKE

Thanks, man.

ROB

No problem, buddy. You eat anything today?

Mike shakes his head "no."

ROB

Yesterday?

Mike shakes his head again.

ROB

You haven't been drinking, have you?

MIKE

No. Just O.J.

Rob cuts into the pepperoni with his Swiss army knife. Mike drinks his juice.

MIKE

Sorry about what happened at the Dresden. I had no
idea . . .

ROB

Don't sweat it. Now I got an L.A. gun story. You
should hear the way I tell it to the guys back home. He
had an Uzi.

Mike half-smiles.

Beat.

ROB

You want to talk about it?

MIKE

What's the point?

ROB

It's been two days. You should call that girl Nikki . . .

Mike grabs his head in pain.

MIKE

Uuuuugh!

ROB

Oh boy.

MIKE

I'm such an asshole.

ROB

She wasn't your type anyway.

Beat.

MIKE

I think I'm gonna move Back East.

ROB

Well, *that's* dumb.

MIKE

What's dumb about it?

ROB

Well, you're doing so well . . .

MIKE

How am I doing well? I host an open mike and I played a fuckin' bus driver in a movie. Big fuckin' deal. I'm with an agency that specializes in fuckin' magicians. How *good* am I doing?

ROB

At least you didn't get turned down for Goofy . . .

MIKE

They turned you down?

ROB

They went for someone with more theme park experience. I woulda killed for that job.

Mike lets it sink in.

ROB

See, it's all how you look at it. If your life sucks, then mine is god-awful. I mean, I moved out here partially because I saw how well you were doing. You got in the union, you got an agent. I thought if you could make it, maybe I could too . . .

MIKE

I didn't make it . . .

ROB

That's your problem, man. You can't see what you've got, only what you've lost. Those guys are right. You are money.

Mike smiles, then . . .

MIKE
(starting to cry)
Then why won't she call . . . ?

ROB
Because you left, man. She's got her own world to deal
with in New York. She was a sweet girl, but fuck her.
You gotta move on. You gotta let go of the past. The
future is so beautiful. Every day is so sunny out here.
It's like Manifest Destiny man. I mean, we made it.
What's past is prologue. That which does not kill us
makes us stronger. All that shit. You'll get over it.

MIKE
How did you get over it? I mean, how long till it
stopped hurting?

ROB
Sometimes it still hurts. You know how it is, man. I
mean, each day you think about it less and less. And
then one day you wake up and you don't think of it at
all, and you almost miss that feeling. It's kinda weird.
You miss the pain.

*We see that Mike has been GNAWING AWAY at Rob's pepperoni and
semolina as he listens intently.*

MIKE
You *miss* the pain?

ROB
. . . for the same reason you miss her. You lived with it
so long.

MIKE
Wow.
(finishing the loaf)
You wanna grab a bite?

> **ROB**
> *(smiling)*

Sure.

He helps Mike up.

CUT TO:

EXT. SUE'S APARTMENT—OUTSIDE THE DOOR—NIGHT

Trent opens the door. He sees Mike standing there dressed for trouble. His face lights up.

> **TRENT**
> Mikey! Guys, Mikey's here!

> **GUYS**
> *(offscreen)*
> *(from the living room)*
> Mikey!

Mike HEARS the sound of a hotly contested SEGA MATCH.

> **SUE**
> *(offscreen)*
> Bitch! You little bitch!

The CAMERA follows Mike and Trent into the . . .

INT. LIVING ROOM—SUE'S APARTMENT—NIGHT

Mike's JAW DROPS when he sees that Sue has been playing hockey against the BALD GUY from the Dresden.

BALD GUY

Bitch! You bitch!

The room is filled with the BALD GUY'S CREW. They greet Mike as they take hits off their forty ouncers.

SUE

Trent. Take over.

They do the high-speed "controller handoff."

Sue crosses to Mike.

SUE

I'm *so sorry*, man. I was out of line.

MIKE

What are they *doing* here?

SUE

We ran into them that night at Roscoe's. Tee cleared it up, I apologized, bought them some chicken and waffles. They fuckin' *love* Tee. That boy can talk.

All the baldies howl and slap hands at Tee's snappy bits.

SUE

But most important, man, I'm sorry about what I said. I was drunk . . . My adrenaline was going . . .

MIKE

Don't sweat it, man. I needed a kick in the ass. We're better friends for it.

SUE

Thanks, man.
                    (they hug)
I've been hating myself for the last two days.

MIKE

Believe me, I know what that's like.
                    (then to Trent)
Yo, Double Down! What time are we leaving?

TRENT
Five minutes, baby. Hey, it's been two days. You should
call Nikki and see if she wants to meet you there.

CUT TO:
**EXT. THE DERBY—HOLLYWOOD
NIGHTCLUB—NIGHT**

*The THREE SWINGERS walk past the line. They greet the doorman as
they enter the service entrance in a Scorsese-style STEADICAM SHOT,
which continues up the stairs and through the kitchen into . . .*

**INT. THE DERBY—HOLLYWOOD
NIGHTCLUB—NIGHT**

*They enter the domed deco lounge and the full house parts for them and greets
them in perfect Scorsese choreography.*

They pass the billiard table and the circular brass-rail bar.

*The six-piece swing band decked out in zoot suits wail on stage as the crowded
dance floor whirls.*

The swingers eventually settle into a dark curtained-off onstage booth.

Sue thrusts a scotch into Mike's hand.

INT. THE DERBY—MONTAGE—NIGHT

Montage of smoking, drinking, and carousing.

The parquet floor is packed with swinging hipsters dressed in Hollywood's

take on forties threads. The dancing is full-blown overcrowded slam swing.
The floor is full, and everyone is damn good. This definitely ain't amateur
night.

INT. BAR AREA—THE DERBY—NIGHT

Mike steps up to the bar to refill his drink. He sees a WOMAN
(LORRAINE) sitting at the bar.

She's cute.

Real cute.

She glows.

There's something fresh about her. She's dressed nice, but different. She
definitely is not a regular.

She throws Mike a half-smile, then looks away.

He looks away.

Should he?

He shakes his head to himself. No.

Beat.

He looks over at her again.

Mike's P.O.V. of a WHITE BUNNY sitting on a bar stool.

He smiles, shrugs, and CROSSES TO HER.

When he gets to her she has reverted back to human form.

MIKE

Hi.

LORRAINE

Hi.

MIKE

I'm Mike.

LORRAINE

Hi, Mike. I'm Lorraine.

MIKE

Like the quiche?

LORRAINE
(gentle sarcasm)
That's a new one. Yes. Like the quiche.

MIKE

I like quiche.

LORRAINE

I thought real men don't like quiche.

MIKE

My reputation seems to have preceded me.

LORRAINE

Why? You're not a real man?

MIKE

Not lately.

MATCH CUT TO:

Trent points the conversation out to Sue from across the room.

Trent and Sue's P.O.V. of Mike and Lorraine having an unforced, enjoyable conversation.

TRENT

It's *on* . . .

SUE

. . . it's on.

MATCH CUT TO:
BACK IN THE TRENCHES:

LORRAINE
. . . so I thought, what the hell, they make movies in
L.A., not in Michigan, so I moved here.

MIKE
Just like that?

LORRAINE
Well, it wasn't that simple, but yeah.

MIKE
How was it hard?

LORRAINE
Well, I left someone very special behind.

MIKE
Tell me about it . . .

LORRAINE
You too?

MIKE
Yeah.

LORRAINE
(lights up)
I thought I was going to die.

MIKE
It's been six months and I'm just starting to get over it.

LORRAINE

Oh, God. That's two more than me. Tell me it gets
better.

MIKE
(smiles)

It does.

LORRAINE

How?

MIKE

Don't get me wrong, it still sucks, but you start to see
that there are advantages to being single.

LORRAINE
(coyly)

Like what?

MIKE

What what? What advantages?

LORRAINE

You said there are advantages to being single. I want to
know what the advantages are.

MIKE
(playing along)

Well . . . You can talk to a woman at a bar without
worrying if anyone's watching you.

CUT TO:

Trent and Sue are watching from across the room.

TRENT

It's on.

SUE

. . . it's definitely on.

BACK TO:

LORRAINE

What else?

MIKE

What else . . . ? Let's see . . . You have complete
freedom.

LORRAINE

To do what?

MIKE

I don't know . . . To grow, to go out. Whatever you
want.

LORRAINE

Anything?

MIKE

Anything.

LORRAINE

Like if I meet a handsome young man and I wanted to
ask him to dance? I can do that?

MIKE

Uh, if the guy wanted to.

LORRAINE

You don't think the guy would find me attractive
enough to dance with?

MIKE

Yes. I mean, no. I mean, maybe he would find her, I

mean, you, attractive. Maybe he doesn't like to dance. Maybe all he likes to do is just stand around and drink and smoke and look cool with his buddies who don't dance either . . .

LORRAINE

Maybe it doesn't matter if he's a good dancer 'cause it's a slow song, if that's what he's afraid of.

MIKE
(smirk)

No . . . Maybe that's not the case. Maybe she shouldn't be such a smug little shit because she'd be surprised at what a good dancer he really is, but it's been a long time and he doesn't know if he wants . . .

LORRAINE

Mike . . .

She gets up. She's beautiful. She is beautiful.

LORRAINE

. . . Will you dance with me?

She's in great shape, and look how classy her vintage dress looks. A vision from the forties. She's too good for this place. She belongs on the nose of a B–52. What can he say, but . . .

MIKE

Sure I will.

He awkwardly leads her to the unusually empty dance floor. They START TO DANCE. It's a slow song and they boringly rock back and forth. Mike is self-conscious, but her touch. Oh, her touch.

CUT TO:

Trent and Sue watching in disbelief.

SUE

It is *on*.

TRENT

. . . it is *so* on.

BACK TO:

The couple's dance is cut short as there were only a few bars left of the slow ballad. Mike smiles politely in relief and begins to lead Lorraine off the floor.

She pulls him back. He's not getting off that easy. She wants a whole song. He politely holds her, poised for another slow number. They're alone on the floor.

Much to Mike's dismay, the song begins with a DRIVING TOM-TOM SOLO. This cues every hep cat in the Derby that the big one's coming. The zoot-suiters flood the floor for the last dance of the night.

Mike pleadingly shakes his head at Lorraine. It's too fast. Her eyes narrow as her grip tightens. No sympathy here.

The band breaks into the full-tilt swing number and the dance floor writhes around them.

They stand motionless for what seems like an eternity.

Gut check. Fuck it. Sink or swim.

Mike grabs her like a man grabs a woman. It's just a simple six-count swing step, but they're in perfect harmony.

Mike and Lorraine look into each other's eyes. It's on, baby.

As Mike's courage grows, the moves start to flow. A spin at first. Then a double twirl. It's not long before he's throwing her through combinations that stand out even among the pros.

CUT TO:

Trent and Sue, mouths agape.

BACK TO:

Mike is whipping her smoothly through violent-looking combinations without a trace of hesitation, and, boy, can she follow.

The set ends with a flourishing crescendo. They're frozen in a final dip, panting through a glaze of clean sweat.

Mike and Lorraine smile and look into each other's eyes. The smile slowly disappears. Will they kiss?

They're close.

Really close.

Lips almost touching.

Mike tries to muster up the courage, but it's been so long.

He can't do it. He lets her up.

The floor clears. Exhausted dancers push past them. Forget it. The moment's gone.

What the hell. They had a great time. What's the hurry?

SOFT CUT TO:
EXT. HILLHURST AVE.—OUTSIDE THE DERBY—NIGHT

Mike is walking Lorraine to her car. They come upon a parked Escort.

LORRAINE

Well . . . This is it.

MIKE

Listen. I had a great time.

LORRAINE

Me too.

MIKE

I would love to see you again sometime.

LORRAINE

I'll be around.

MIKE

That's not good enough. I want to make plans to see you.

LORRAINE

Let me get a pen out of my car.
(opens the door)
Do you have something to write on?

Mike hands her a business card.

LORRAINE
(looking at it)

You're a comedian?

MIKE

Yeah. And an actor.

LORRAINE

I'll have to come see you sometime.

MIKE

If and when I get a real gig I'll call you.

LORRAINE

It's not going too well?

MIKE

When I lived in New York they made it sound like they were giving out sitcoms to stand-ups at the airport. I got off the plane in L.A. six months ago and all I got to show for it is a tan.

LORRAINE

Didn't you tell me to be patient with my career?

MIKE

. . . Yeah, but entertainment law isn't something you just jump into . . .

LORRAINE

Neither is acting. Not if you're serious about it.
(She writes her number on the card.)
Can I have one of these?

MIKE

Why, you like the duck with the cigar?
(hands her a card)

LORRAINE

Yeah. Nice touch. It's the logo from *You Bet Your Life*, right?

MIKE

Good eye. Not one club owner got it. They all ask me why I got Donald Duck on my card.

LORRAINE

Hey, at least it's not Goofy.

Beat.

LORRAINE

Well, I should be getting . . .

MIKE

. . . It's really getting late.

LORRAINE

. . . home. It's getting late. Yeah.

Beat.

LORRAINE

Can I give you a ride to your car . . . ?

MIKE

. . . Nah. I'm right across the street . . .

LORRAINE

. . . Which one . . . ?

MIKE

. . . The red piece of shit over there . . .

LORRAINE

. . . well, it suits you . . .

MIKE

. . . get the hell outta here already . . .

Mike leans in and slowly gives her the sweetest, softest, most innocent kiss.

He backs up. She's got that goofy look as she unlocks her club. The horn accidentally HONKS as she pulls it off, breaking the silence. She rolls her eyes and they share a smile. She starts the car.

LORRAINE

Bye.

She drives off. Cute wave.

He watches her go.

DISSOLVE TO:
INT. HOLLYWOOD HILLS
DINER—WINDOW BOOTH—SAME NIGHT

Mike, Trent, and Sue eat a late-night breakfast. Trent has too much food in front of him, and too much booze inside him.

The WAITRESS finishes serving their plates.

TRENT

Thank you, darling. This looks wonderful . . .

Trent abruptly jumps, reacting as though Mike has KICKED HIM under the table. The ANGLE of the SHOT reveals that he's faking it.

TRENT
(angrily to Mike)
All right! I'll ask!
(then to waitress)
Where do all the high school girls hang out?

The waitress throws Mike a disgusted look. Mike just shakes his head in resignation and turns red. She walks off.

TRENT

You were off your ass back there!
(to waitress)
Don't forget my oatmeal, gorgeous!
(to Mike)
Where the hell did you learn to do all that twirly whirly shit!?!

MIKE

Shh . . . Keep it down, Jackknife. I took a ballroom class with Michelle. I never danced with anyone but her, till tonight. That Lorraine chick is *good*.

TRENT

You were good!!! Shhh . . . Did you see how she was vibing you?

SUE

Sorry, man.

TRENT

Yeah. You probably coulda hit that tonight if you didn't have to drive us home.

SUE

. . . Definitely . . .

MIKE

It's not like that . . .

TRENT

Don't give me that! She *liked* you, man!!!

MIKE

Easy, shh . . . I know she liked me. I mean, it's not like
I wanted to do anything with her tonight.

SUE

Good for you, man. He's being smart.

MIKE

She's really special, guys.

TRENT

The bear's got his claws back.
                    (yelling to waitress)
He has his *claws*!
                    (to Mike)
Shh . . . I know.

SUE

Be smart about it.

TRENT

I'm telling you. Wait *three* days, baby.

SUE

You don't have to wait *three* days . . .

TRENT

. . . Okay, two . . . .

SUE

. . . just be smart about it.

MIKE

Guys . . . Guys . . . I got it under control.

TRENT

Oh. He's got it under *control* . . .

SUE

. . . Well, then, I guess we don't have to worry about *him* anymore.

TRENT
(yelling to the waitress)
Our little baby's *all growds up*!!!

He smirks and shakes his head.

MIKE

You're such an asshole. Why do you always have to embarrass me by putting on a major production whenever we're in public?

Trent enthusiastically jumps up and spins and spots like a ballerina.

TRENT

All growds up . . . All growds up . . All growds up!

CUT TO:
EXT. HOLLYWOOD HILLS DINER—LONG SHOT THROUGH THE WINDOW—SAME

Trent climbs onto the table with a napkin on his head. He is carrying on about something M.O.S. Mike and Sue laugh their asses off as the manager tries to coax him down. Alcohol is a terrible drug.

DISSOLVE TO:
INT. MIKE'S APARTMENT—NIGHT

Mike is standing in the middle of the room looking at LORRAINE'S NUMBER on the back of the BUSINESS CARD.

He looks at the clock.

2:45 A.M.

He looks back at the NUMBER.

Beat.

He thinks better of it. He wedges it into a crack in the answering machine and unbuttons his shirt for bed . . .

> **ANSWERING MACHINE**
> *(synthesized voice)*
>
> Good move.
>
> > *Mike smirks.*

FADE TO:
**INT. MIKE'S APARTMENT—THE
NEXT MORNING**

An alarm wakes Mike, who pops up with a perky yawn. Frank sings "Sweet Lorraine." It looks like a bright and sunny morning with the birds singing. The clock reveals, however, that it is well past noon.

He walks to the phone and pulls the CARD out of the crack.

He sticks it back in the crack.

He makes an "x" on a day of his calendar.

Mike stares at the card with Lorraine's number, then the calender with one "x" on it, then at the phone, then the clock, card, phone, calender, clock, time passes, card, not yet, phone, clock, time passes, cuts repeat and quicken, until, finally . . .

He is startled by the phone ringing.

He forces himself to wait another ring and a half to pick up.

MIKE

Hello?

FEMALE VOICE
(voice-over)

Hi, Michael.

MIKE

Michelle?

MICHELLE
(voice-over)

How's it going? It's been a while . . .

MIKE

. . . Six months.

MICHELLE
(voice-over)

How are you doing?

MIKE

Fine . . . I guess. You?

MICHELLE
(voice-over)

Good.
(long pause)

I think about things.

MIKE

Yeah?

MICHELLE
(voice-over)

Yeah.

MIKE

What kind of things?

MICHELLE
(voice-over)

You know, us.

MIKE

I thought you met someone else.

MICHELLE
(voice-over)

It doesn't matter. I think about you every day.

MIKE

Really?

MICHELLE
(voice-over)

I miss you, Mike.

MIKE

Why didn't you call?

MICHELLE
(voice-over)

I couldn't. Do you know how hard it's been not to call you? I pick up the phone every night. Whenever that commercial comes on . . .

MIKE

. . . the Micheline commercial . . .

MICHELLE
(voice-over)

. . . Yeah, with the baby in the tire. One time I started to cry right in front of Pierre . . .

MIKE

Pierre . . . That's his name? Pierre? Is he French?

MICHELLE
(voice-over)

No, he's not . . . Listen I don't want to talk about him.

That's a whole other headache. I called because I heard you might be moving back to Queens . . .

The BEEP of Mike's CALL WAITING.

MIKE
Hang on. Let me get rid of this call.

He clicks to the OTHER LINE.

MIKE
Hello?

LORRAINE
Hi, Mike?

MIKE
Lorraine?

LORRAINE
Are you on the other line?

MIKE
Yeah, hold on.

LORRAINE
I can call back . . .

MIKE
No, no. Hold on.

He clicks back to the OTHER LINE.

MIKE
Hi.

MICHELLE
(voice-over)
I heard you might be moving back . . .

MIKE
Yeah, uh, I don't think that's gonna be happening any

time soon . . . Listen, can I call you right back? I gotta
take this call . . .

MICHELLE
(voice-over)

I'm going out of town for a week. The cab's on its way.
Can't you talk for five minutes?

MIKE

I really want to catch up with you, but I've gotta take
this call. They're holding. I'll talk to you when you get
back in town. Bye.

MICHELLE
(voice-over)

Good-bye. I lov . . . (click)

Mike SWITCHES LINES, cutting Michelle off midsentence.

MIKE

Hi. Sorry about that.

LORRAINE

You didn't have to get off the other line. I would've
called you back.

MIKE

That's okay. I wanted to talk to you.

*The answering machine flashes an LED and gives a happy R2D2 beep.
Mike smiles at his old friend and holds a finger to his lips.*

LORRAINE
(voice-over)

Listen, Mike. You really didn't have to get off the line.
I just wanted to ask you one thing. I know I shouldn't
have called, I mean, my friends said I should wait two
days . . . Oh God, I probably sound like such a
schoolgirl . . .

A CLOSE-UP of Mike's face. All tension is released. Relief washes over him as he realizes that his burden has been lifted.

He's free.

> **LORRAINE**
> *(voice-over)*
> It's just that it's tonight only . . . I mean, it's Sinatra's birthday and they have this thing every year at the Room. Do you know where that is? It's impossible to find if you've never been there. I don't understand why none of the clubs in Hollywood have signs. Anyway, I'm so bad at this, if you're not busy I thought you might . . .

As the dialogue fades out, then we . . .

FADE TO:
INT. HOLLYWOOD HILLS DINER—DAY

Fade up on Mike's peaceful face. Trent speaks in a gravelly voice from OFFSCREEN.

> **TRENT**
> Wait, wait. You hung up with which one?

> **MIKE**
> Michelle.

We now see Trent sitting across from him. He does not look good. His chin rests in his hands, which are completely covered with the blue ink from dozens of club stamps. He inhales coffee steam.

> **TRENT**
> *(hung over)*
> You hung up with your girlfriend.

> **MIKE**
> Ex.

TRENT

Oh, now she's your "ex"?

MIKE

She always been my "ex".

TRENT

Yeah, sure. Dude, you hung up on her?

MIKE

I wanted to take the other call.

TRENT

So you called right back?

MIKE

No.

TRENT

Why not?

MIKE

I don't know. It didn't occur to me.

TRENT

Wait a minute. You're telling me you spend six months
of your life tearing yourself apart over this chick, and
she calls you and you take another call?

MIKE

Yeah.

TRENT

Why?

MIKE

I kept asking myself the same question, then, when I
was walking over here, it hit me, and it's so simple. It
all comes down to this . . . :

*Trent perks up as he notices a BEAUTIFUL BABY making eye contact
with him from two booths down. She's sitting alone.*

TRENT
(interrupts Mike)
Dude. I'm getting vibed in a weird way. Shit. Who the hell is that? She's looking at me like she knows me.

MIKE
You don't recognize her?

TRENT
Oh, Mikey, who the hell knows. I mighta met her out one night with Sue and told her I was a race car driver or something . . .

The beautiful baby mouths "Hi."

TRENT
(mouths back "Hi")
No way I met her before. I would definitely remember *her*.

The vibing escalates gradually until she actually starts to play PEEK-A-BOO with a big toothy grin. Trent is right in there, looking as silly as she does.

MIKE
What the hell is going on?
(sneaks a look)

TRENT
Stop, stop. Don't look, man. I've never met a girl with this much confidence.
(talking trash under his breath)
You're a sweetie. Yeah, peek-a-boo, baby. Have some of this, you little party girl.

Mike smiles and shakes his head.

Their body language to each other grows to ridiculous exaggeration, until she finally gets up to approach their table.

TRENT
Be cool, man. She's coming over.

She stops short at the other seat across from her and reveals that she was actually making baby talk to a TWO YEAR OLD sitting with her whose head was hidden by the high seat back, perfectly matching Trent's eyeline.

She picks the baby up and passes Trent, who she never even noticed.

Trent looks at Mike, temporarily humbled. Mike throws him a warm smile.

Sinatra's STRING SECTION fades up.

Mike turns to look out into the sunshine. He's lost in his own world.

CUT TO:

CLOSE UP of Mike through the glass. He's a new man.

The lyrics of "Witchcraft" kick in as we TILT UP to:

EXT. HOLLYWOOD—DAY

The daylight turns the nocturnal playground into a sweet paradise. It's a new day in Hollywood.

The air is clear like a day after rain.

We see the snowy-white letters nestled in the green-peppered mountainside as we . . .

FADE TO WHITE

THE SWINGERS RULES
by Vince Vaughn and Jon Favreau

RULE # I

THERE ARE NO RULES

TRENT

She *smiled*, baby.

MIKE

I can't believe what an asshole you are.

TRENT

Did she, or did she not smile?

MIKE

She was smiling at what an asshole you are.

TRENT

She was smiling at how *money* I am, what I did with
her.

The bottom line is make genuine contact at all costs. If you connect on a
genuine level, you have the ball. Shake it up and have fun. Everyone is bored
and sick of the bullshit. An honest moment of connection is refreshing.

TEAM PLAY

TRENT

Baby, this is what we came here for. We met a beautiful baby and she likes you.

MIKE

She likes *you*.

TRENT

Whatever. We'll see. Daddy's gonna get her to bring a friend. We'll both get one. I don't care if I'm with her or one of her beautiful baby friends.

There's plenty to go around. If you hog the ball, the team loses. Your friends are not your adversaries. Work together and everyone wins. Petty competition makes everyone look bad. Worst of all, you look desperate and bitter. Nobody likes desperate or bitter. Everyone likes fun. Keep it fun. It's fun to share.

RULE #3

LESS IS MORE

TRENT

I just stare at their mouth and crinkle my brow and
somehow I turn out to be the big sweetie.

People like to fill in the blanks. People also want things to be perfect. Keep
your mouth shut and they'll fill in the blanks perfectly. Don't try to guess what
they're looking for. It's not about what you say, it's about how you listen.
Listen.

WOMEN AREN'T DUMB

MIKE

That was so fuckin' *money*. It was like that "Jedi mind"
shit.

TRENT

That's what I'm telling you, baby. The babies love that
stuff. They don't want all that sensitive shit. You start
talking to them about puppy dogs and ice cream. They
know what you *want*. What do you think? You think
they don't know?

MIKE

I know. I know.

TRENT

They know what you want, believe me. Pretending is
just a waste of time. You're gonna take them there
eventually anyway. Don't apologize for it.

Women are smart. Take this into consideration. They're good at reading the
vibe and are in tune with what's really going down. They know what's
happening. Don't manipulate, deny, and condescend. It's insulting.

RULE #5

BE HONEST

MIKE

I'm just trying to be a gentleman, show some
respect . . .

TRENT

Respect, my ass. What they respect is honesty. You see
how they dress when they go out? They want to be
noticed. You're just showing them it's working. You
gotta get off this respect kick, baby. There ain't nothing
wrong with letting them know that you're money and
that you want to party.

Women like attention. It's flattering as long as you're respectful and honest.
Formalities are not nearly as important as respecting their intelligence.

Be honest with yourself and with them. If you want intimacy, then own up to
it. Don't come at them like you're interested in their nail polish if what you
really want is intimacy. It's insulting. You're a man, she's a woman. Deal with
it. The more you pretend that it's not about sexual attraction, the harder it
will be to redefine the parameters. Honesty works like magic if you're free
from guilt. The truth shall set you free.

RULE #6

IF YOU MUST LIE,
KEEP IT SIMPLE

CHRISTY

What do you guys do?

MIKE

I'm a comedian.

LISA

Do you ever perform out here? I'd love to see you.

MIKE

No . . .

LISA

You should. A lot of comics play Vegas.

MIKE

Well, I'm afraid it's not that easy . . .

LISA

Why not?

MIKE

There are different circuits . . . it's hard to explain . . .
you wouldn't understand . . .

LISA

Who's your booking agent?

MIKE
(flustered)

Oh? You know about booking agents . . . I don't, uh, actually have a *West Coast* agent as of yet . . .

LISA

Well, who represents you Back East?

MIKE

Actually, it's funny you . . . I'm actually, uh, *between* . . .

LISA

What do you do, Trent?

TRENT

I'm a producer.

BOTH GIRLS

Wow . . . Oooh . . . Ahhh . . .

Lying is bad. Forget the ethical issue, it's bad business. It demonstrates a lack of self-confidence. Even if you get away with it, you're going down the wrong road.

But if a friend gets in trouble, sometimes a simple lie can be a perfect parachute.

RULE #7

SETTING THE TONE

MIKE

She didn't like me, anyway.

TRENT

She thought you were money.

MIKE

I don't think so.

TRENT

I heard them talking. They both thought you were
money.

MIKE

Yeah, a good friend.

Trent turns off the car and turns to face Mike.

TRENT

Baby, you take your*self* out of the game. You start
talking about puppy dogs and ice cream, of course it's
gonna be on the friend tip.

You're a man, so present yourself as one. Confidence and being comfortable
with one's self is very attractive. So if you're attracted to a beautiful baby, be
both confident and comfortable with that. Don't apologize or qualify how
you're feeling. She'll respect you for it.

RULE #8

TIMING IS EVERYTHING

MIKE

What time's this party tonight?

TRENT

It starts at eight . . .

SUE

. . . which means no one will get there till ten.

MIKE

So, what? Eleven?

TRENT AND SUE

Midnight.

There's nothing like a good entrance. You wouldn't want to sit at a table that wasn't set. If you're there too early, you look desperate. Show up late like you're "just stopping by," and you come off like the man about town.

DEER IN THE HEADLIGHTS

> **TRENT**
> What are you doing?

> **MIKE**
> What?

> **TRENT**
> You looked *right at* her, baby.

> **MIKE**
> She didn't notice.

> **SUE**
> Yes she did.

> **TRENT**
> Damn. Now I gotta go in early.

> **MIKE**
> I'm sorry.

> **TRENT**
> Don't sweat it, baby. This ones a layup.

Everyone wants a mystery. Staring deadpan at a beautiful baby cheats her out of the suspense and courtship she deserves. Keep it intriguing and give her the gift of a challenge.

THE LAW OF THE JUNGLE

TRENT

You're like this big bear with claws and fangs . . .

SUE

. . . and big fuckin' teeth . . .

TRENT

. . . and teeth . . . And she's like this little bunny
cowering in the corner . . .

SUE

. . . shivering . . .

TRENT

. . . And you're just looking at your claws like "How
do I kill this bunny? . . ."

SUE

. . . You're just poking at it . . .

TRENT

. . . Yeah. You're just gently batting it around . . . and
the rabbit's all scared . . .

SUE

. . . and you got big claws and fangs . . .

TRENT

. . . and fangs . . . and you're like "I don't know what
to do. How do I kill this bunny? . . ."

SUE

. . . you're like a big bear.

The strongest will survives. Don't waste your time filling your head with self-
doubt. The competition's fierce, so always give yourself the edge. A sense of
self-respect makes all the difference in the world. You can be the king of the
jungle or just another hyena cowering at the water hole. It's all up to you.

BE A BAD MAN

TRENT
(pulling him aside, dead serious)
Now when you talk to her, I don't want you to be the
guy in the PG–13 movie that everyone really hopes
makes it happen. I want you to be the guy in the rated
R movie who you're not sure if you like yet.

Don't hide the fact that you like sex. That doesn't mean to act like the fourteen
year old on the back of the bus who's constantly pulling on himself and making
obscene noises. It just means own your sexuality and don't apologize for it.

RULE #12
THE WAITING GAME

CHARLES

Eight-one-eight.

MIKE

Three-one-oh.

Everyone reacts favorably to this area code.

MIKE

How long do I wait to call?

TRENT

A day.

MIKE

Tomorrow?

TRENT

No . . .

SUE

. . . Tomorrow, *then* a day.

TRENT

. . . Yeah.

MIKE

So, two days?

TRENT

Yeah. I guess you could call it that.

SUE

Definitely. Two days. That's the industry standard . . .

TRENT

(to Sue, shop talk)

. . . I used to wait two days. Now everyone waits two days. Three days is kinda the money now, don't you think?

SUE

. . . Yeah. But two's enough not to look anxious . . .

TRENT

Yeah, but three days is kinda the money . . .

MIKE

(interrupting sarcastically)

Why don't I just wait three weeks and tell her I was cleaning out my wallet and found her number . . .

CHARLES

. . . then ask where you met her . . .

MIKE

Yeah, I'll tell her I don't remember and then I'll ask what she looks like.

(pause)

Then I'll ask if we fucked. How's that, Tee? Is that "the money"?

The guys laugh.

TRENT

Laugh all you want, but if you call too soon you can scare off a nice baby who's ready to party.

SUE

Don't listen to him. You call whenever it feels right to you.

MIKE

How long are you guys gonna wait to call your honeys?

TRENT & SUE

Six days.

Be a man with a slow hand. The ladies love foreplay, and that's exactly why you wait a few days before you call. No reason to rush it. Let her savor the wait. She'll thank you later.

RULE #13

GRACE UNDER PRESSURE

NIKKI
(recorded)
Hi. This is Nikki. Leave a message.
(beep)

MIKE
Hi, Nikki. This is Mike. I met you tonight at the
Dresden. I, uh, just called to say I, uh, had a really great
time and you should call me tomorrow, or, like, in two
days, whatever. My number is 213-555-4679 . . .
(beep)

Mike hangs up.

Beat.

He dials again.

NIKKI
(recorded)
Hi. This is Nikki. Leave a message.
(beep)

MIKE
Hi, Nikki. This is Mike, again. I just called because it
sounded like your machine might've cut me off before
I gave you my number, and also to say sorry for calling

so late, but you were still there when I left the Dresden,
so I knew I'd get your machine. Anyway, my number
is . . .

(beep)

Mike calls back right away.

NIKKI
(recorded)
Hi. This is Nikki. Leave a message.
(beep)

MIKE
213-555-4679. That's all. I just wanted to leave my
number. I don't want you to think I'm weird, or
desperate or something . . .
(he regrets saying it immediately)
. . . I mean, you know, we should just hang out. That's
it. No expectations. Just, you know, hang out. Bye.
(beep)

He hangs up.

Beat.

He dials.

NIKKI
(recorded)
Hi. This is Nikki. Leave a message.
(beep)

MIKE
I just got out of a six-year relationship. Okay? That
should help explain why I'm acting so weird. It's not
you. It's me. I just wanted to say that. Sorry.
(pause)
This is Mike.
(beep)

He dials again. There's no turning back.

NIKKI
(recorded)

Hi. This is Nikki. Leave a message.
(beep)

MIKE

Hi, Nikki. This is Mike again. Could you just call me
when you get in? I'll be up for a while, and I'd just
rather talk to you in person instead of trying to squeeze
it all . . .

(beep)

Fuck!

He dials yet again.

NIKKI
(recorded)

Hi. This is Nikki. Leave a message.
(beep)

MIKE

Hi, Nikki. Mike. I don't think this is working out. I
think you're great, but maybe we should just take some
time off from each other. It's not you, really. It's me.
It's only been six months . . .

NIKKI
(Live, in person. She picks up the line.)

Mike?

MIKE

Nikki! Great! Did you just walk in, or were you
listening all along?

NIKKI
(calmly)

Don't call me ever again.

MIKE

Wow, I guess you were home . . .
(click)

Our generation is the first to be presented with the challenge of the answering machine. A good message can put you on the fast track to paradise, a bad one can lead to public ridicule and endless playbacks to the delight of family and friends. The stakes are high. This is no joke.

The golden rule is keep it simple. Don't try to overexplain who you are or how you're feeling. It's a moment frozen in amber. It's a small piece of your soul. Give her a taste—the little pink spoon, not the whole sundae.

RULE # 14

SKIP THE BIRDSEED

LORRAINE

Well . . . This is it.

MIKE

Listen. I had a great time.

LORRAINE

Me too.

MIKE

I would love to see you again sometime.

LORRAINE

I'll be around.

MIKE

That's not good enough. I want to make plans to see you.

LORRAINE

Let me get a pen out of my car.
(opens the door)
Do you have something to write on?

Sometimes it just happens. Let it. Don't let stupid rules from a book get in the way. If you're lucky enough to have things unfold organically, don't ruin it. You're money.

RULE #15

TRUST YOURSELF

SUE

Sorry, man.

TRENT

Yeah. You probably coulda hit that tonight if you didn't have to drive us home.

SUE

. . . Definitely . . .

MIKE

It's not like that . . .

TRENT

Don't give me that! She *liked* you, man!!!

MIKE

Easy, shh . . . I know she liked me. I mean, it's not like I wanted to do anything with her tonight.

SUE

Good for you, man. He's being smart.

MIKE

Guys . . . Guys . . . I got it under control.

TRENT

Oh. He's got it under *control* . . .

SUE

. . . Well, then, I guess we don't have to worry about *him* anymore.

TRENT

(yelling to the waitress)
Our little baby's *all growds up*!!!

You're always better off trusting your instincts and playing your game. You wouldn't ask Stockton to bang the boards for rebounds and you wouldn't want Shaq trying to drain threes. Stick with what feels right. That way, even if you fail, you've learned something. Trust your instincts and think for yourself.

SWINGERS GLOSSARY

TERMS:

SWINGERS:

    (noun, plural) individuals who share a proclivity for leisure activities
(in the spirit of the "Rat Pack")

MONEY:

    (adj.) top shelf (e.g., "You're *money*.")

BABY:

    1. *(noun)* girl or woman (e.g., "Look at all the beautiful *babies*.")

    2. *(noun)* a term of endearment for a close personal friend

VIBE:

    1. *(verb, transitive)* acting in a manner that suggests interest (e.g., "I
think she's *vibing* you.")

    2. *(noun)* atmosphere or attitude (e.g., "This place has a great
vibe.")

PARTY:

    1. *(verb, intransitive)* to engage in markedly heterosexual activities
(e.g., "She's dressed like she wants to *party*.")

    2. *(adj.)* exemplifying a proclivity for heterosexual activities (e.g.,
"I hear she's a *party* girl.")

    3. *(noun)* social gathering

PUPPY DOGS AND ICE CREAM:

    (adj. or noun) refers to any topic of safe, meaningless conversation
used when someone is afraid to come to terms with their sexual
desires (e.g., "The money babies were throwing him the party
vibes but he was all *puppy dogs and ice cream*.")

SHAQED:

    (verb, transitive) to be rejected in one's sexual advances in a decisive

and forthright manner (e.g., "I was *Shaqed* before I could buy her a drink.")

BUSINESS CLASS:

> *(adj.)* possessing a large enough posterior to necessitate flight arrangements other than coach seating (e.g., "She's got a beautiful face, but she's *business class*.")

ROUNDER:

> *(noun)* one who has been around and possesses life experience. opposite of square

WING MAN/WINGER:

> *(noun)* teammate who assists in a scoring drive

DIGITS:

> *(noun, plural)* phone number

EXPRESSIONS:

"PULL A FREDO":

> Refers to Fredo Corleone "Banging cocktail waitresses two at a time" in *The Godfather*.

"THERE'S THE RUB":

> There's the catch or problem. Borrowed from Hamlet's monologue.

"JEDI MIND SHIT":

> Refers to Obi-Wan Kenobi's ability to influence the weak-minded stormtroopers through use of the Force in *Star Wars*.

CAST AND CREDITS

mike	**JON FAVREAU**
trent	**VINCE VAUGHN**
rob	**RON LIVINGSTON**
sue	**PATRICK VAN HORN**
charles	**ALEX DESERT**
lorraine	**HEATHER GRAHAM**
christy	**DEENA MARTIN**
lisa	**KATHERINE KENDALL**
nikki	**BROOKE LANGTON**
girl with cigar	**BLAKE LINDSLEY**
vegas dealer	**KEVIN JAMES KELLY**
vegas waitress	**STEPHANIE ITTLESON**
$100 gambler	**VERNON VAUGHN**
$5 winner	**JOAN FAVREAU**
peek-a-boo girl	**MADDIE CORMAN**
girl at party	**JAN DYKSTRA**
skully	**RIO HACKFORD**
dresden lounge act	**MARTY & ELAYNE**
derby band	**BIG BAD VOODOO DADDY**
$100 gamblers	**SHERI ROSENBLUM**
	STASEA ROSENBLUM
$5 gambler	**PAMELA SHAW**
pit boss	**TOM ALLEY**
lounge lizard	**REVEREND PHIL DIXON**
bartender	**ASHLEY M. ROGERS**
skully's crew	**JAY DIOLA**
	NICHOLAS GAGLIARDUCCI

	DAVID GOULD
	BILL PHILLIPS
pink dot guy	MENSUR HAMUD
party mystery guy	AHMED AHMED
derby ladies	EUFEMIA PLIMPTON
	MELINDA STARR
dresden ladies	SAMANTHA LEMOLE
	JESSICA BUCHMAN
diner waitress	CAROLINE O'MEARA
derby doormen	GARY AURBACH
	BRAD HALVORSON
diner patrons	CHRISTOPHER A.
	JOYCE
	EDWARD RISSIEN
	JENNA RISSIEN
	MARK SMITH
michelle (in pictures)	TIFFANY KUZON
michelle (voice on phone)	NICOLE LALOGGIA

DERBY DANCERS

JOHN ABRAHAM	JAY DIOLA
RACHEL GALLAGAN	LISA GUERRIERO
THOMAS HALL	DAMIANA KAMISHIN
CURTIS LINDERSMITH	JENNIFER LUCERO
PINKI MARSOLEK	RHONDA MARTIN
MARTINA MIGENES	PAUL MOJICA
SAM MOLLO	JACOB MORRIS
MICHAEL SCOTT	BERNARD SERRANO
ROSALIND SMITH	MOLLY STERN
JOHNNY WALKER	LISA WOLSTEIN

FILMMAKERS

director and director of photography	DOUG LIMAN
producer	VICTOR SIMPKINS
producer/line producer	NICOLE SHAY
	LALOGGIA
writer and co-producer	JON FAVREAU

executive producer	**CARY WOODS**
editor	**STEPHEN MIRRIONE**
production designer	**BRAD HALVORSON**
costume designer	**GENEVIEVE TYRRELL**
music supervisor	**JULIANNE KELLEY**
original score by	**JUSTIN REINHARDT**
production manager	**EDEN H. WURMFELD**
associate producer/production coordinator	**BRADFORD L. SCHLEI**
location manager	**KELLY KINCAID**
associate producer/1st assistant director	**AVRAM LUDWIG**
2nd assistant director	**BRADFORD ''WALLY'' MINNICH**
script supervisors	**TYRONE SCOTT**
	ALEXANDER WELLS
	PAUL ALCUS
1st assistant camera	**LORNA LESLIE**
2nd assistant camera	**SABRINA MERICS**
camera assistant	**SEAN O'CONNOR**
gaffer	**RODERICK SPENCER**
key grip	**VLADIMIR MELNIK**
grip	**MICHAEL PESCASIO**
swing	**STEVE SCARLATA**
still photographers	**JIM TOWNE**
	ARLENE PACHASA
hair and makeup	**ERIC A. POLITO**
	MOLLY R. STERN
art/set dresser	**DAVID GOULD**
art/property master	**DIANA PEDERSON**
wardrobe assistants	**MELINDA STARR**
	KATHLEEN BEATON
	TISH BECKMAN
dance coordinator	**DAMIANA KAMISHIN**
sound mixer	**ALAN B. SAMUELS**
boom operator	**DAVID R. COOK**
production assistants	**ANTHONY BARRIOS**
	JAY DIOLA
	DENEE EDWARDS
	CHRISTOPHE FARBER

	NICHOLAS GAGLIARDUCCI
casting assistant	KATHRYN MARSH
grip and lighting equipment	RODERICK SPENCER
production sound	ALAN B. SAMULES
production vehicles	AVON RENTALS
dolly	CHAPMAN LEONARD STUDIOS
negative cutter	MAGIC FILMWORKS
opticals	TITLE HOUSE
titles	MELROSE TITLE and OPTICAL
insurance	NICHOL MOON ENTERTAINMENT
catering	RITA FLORA KITCHEN
	GAUCHO GRILL
	EAST INDIA GRILL
	JACOPOS
	LA BOTTEGA
assistant editor	AMBER PFEIFFER
apprentice editor	XOCHITL BAEZ
dialogue editor	INGA LARSEN
sound editor	RENEE SABATH
music consultant	BARRY THOMAS
live recording engineer	PAUL DUGRE
re-recording mixers	LARRY BENJAMIN
	ROSS DAVIS
original score by	THE JAZZ JURY
piano	JUSTIN REINHARDT
saxaphone	MANDO DORAME
trumpet	SCOTT STEEN
guitar	JAMES ACHOR
bass	BART SAMOLIS
drums	JOEL ALPER
recording engineer	ALAN HIRSHBERG
re-recording	LASER PACIFIC
additional sound	AVANT-GARDE STUDIOS
	RYDER SOUND
legal services	WEISSMANN, WOLFF, et al.

MIRAMAX FILMS PRESENTS

in association with
INDEPENDENT PICTURES

an
ALFRED SHAY
Production
a
DOUG LIMAN
Film

swingers

JON FAVREAU
VINCE VAUGHN
RON LIVINGSTON
PATRICK VAN HORN
ALEX DESERT
DEENA MARTIN
KATHERINE KENDALL
BROOKE LANGTON
BLAKE LINDSLEY
AND
HEATHER GRAHAM

executive producer
CARY WOODS

music supervisor
JULIANNE KELLEY

composer
JUSTIN REINHARDT

production designer
BRAD HALVORSON

costume designer
GENEVIEVE TYRRELL

edited by
STEPHEN MIRRIONE

associate producers
BRADFORD L. SCHLEI
AVRAM LUDWIG

written and co-produced by
· **JON FAVREAU**

producer/line producer
NICOLE SHAY LALOGGIA

produced by
VICTOR SIMPKINS

directed and photographed by
DOUG LIMAN